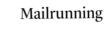

Mailrunning

Mailrunning

three eighteenth-century Atlantic lives

SALLY JEFFERY

TURNEDUP PRESS

Published 2020
Turnedup Press, London

ISBN 978-1-9162221-1-3

A version of this text appeared as a part
of *War stories* by Sally Jeffery, 2019

Printed in England

Front cover: JMW Turner (1775–1851),
*A Stormy Sea and Sky by Daylight,
possibly a study relating to the Eddystone
Lighthouse, c.* 1813
[image © Tate, London 2019]
Back cover: detail from William
Heather's *Chart of the entrances to
Falmouth and Helford,* 1798
[Boston Public Library]

Contents

JMW Turner (1775–1851), *A Stormy Sea and Sky by Daylight, possibly a study relating to the Eddystone Lighthouse, c.* 1813. [© Tate]

Introduction

The spur for trying to throw some light on the story of some ordinary maritime lives came from a brief note on a scrap of paper, written sixty years ago by a retired district commissioner in Mombasa. It was all he had to say about his eighteenth-century ancestor John Philips Boulderson: 'of Boswarren, Cornwall, part owner of Earl of Halifax packet service Falmouth to Virginia'. Once discovered, that small scrap of information could not in the end be left uninvestigated.

During the 1700s and early 1800s, overseas mail from England to the Mediterranean, the West Indies and the Americas was carried by way of the small seaport of Falmouth in the far west of Cornwall. While the journey by road from London to Falmouth was long and slow, an outward Atlantic passage from Falmouth was both shorter and more dependable than sailings from the south coast and channel ports. Vessels heading into the prevailing westerly winds could sail straight out from Falmouth harbour into the wide open water of the ocean. It also put them clear of privateers cruising in the Channel.

The Post Office operated its overseas mail service by contracting with packet boat captains, who provided the boats and crewed them. They were built to a more-or-less standard brig design and sailed to Post Office schedules; in wartime the packets came under military command for the purpose of carrying dispatches. Britain was at war, on and off, from 1740 to 1815, which is the period during which John Boulderson was going to sea. In fact there were three of them: father, son and grandson. All three spent the greater part of their working lives as captains on the Falmouth packet service.

They lived and raised their families in a small English coastal town, but between them they knew the harbours, streets and coffee houses of cities on several continents, and they could navigate oceans. They witnessed at first hand the business of slavery in the Caribbean and South Carolina, and plantation owners often travelled with them as passengers. The packets sailed armed, particularly in wartime, and were under orders to defend the mails to the utmost; usually they did. During a strike in 1810 it was noted of the Falmouth packet seamen: 'it must be recollected that they are always brave & that their gallantry has been conspicuous during the whole of this War'.[1] All three Boulderson packet captains served time in foreign prisons after capture by enemy vessels, in several wars: against the French, then the Americans, the French again, the Americans again.

These men left no first-hand accounts (although one or two other packet sailors did), and there is almost no way other than imagination to envisage the lives their wives and families led. Fortitude must equally have been required of the women who managed their affairs and raised their families alone while the men were at sea, all their futures uncertain. A seventeenth-century puritan preacher in Dartmouth addressing seamen 'sailing Heaven-ward', wrote this: 'I finde it storied of Anacharsis, that when one ask'd him whether the living or dead were more? He returned this answer, You must first tell me (saith he) in which number I must place sea-men'.[2]

Maritime communities probably tended to a more down-to-earth view. While Providence might take a hand, it was their own resourcefulness that would sustain them – especially so at sea, but also on shore. The radical philosopher Mary Wollstonecraft, writing in 1792 about the education of girls, named strength and usefulness as necessary female capabilities.[3] She may not have had many readers in Falmouth, but it was in its way a diverse place. By the 1760s it had a long-established Quaker meeting house, a Baptist church and a synagogue, as well as the parish church where Boulderson lives and deaths were recorded.

This is also a story about news, and how it travels. In the eighteenth century it took at least three weeks for an event on one side of the Atlantic to be heard of on the other, and the same again for the reaction to get back. The time-lag drove the course of politics and of wars. None of these three packet captains signed up for military service – rather the opposite, since packet crews were protected from navy impressment. But they had to fight anyway, to defend the mail from privateers, and throughout these working lives the Georgian wars kept coming, one after another, the American revolutionary war not the least of them.

The lives of apparently unremarkable people such as these tend to be laid open only when they catch the attention of governments. The American revolution has left us views from both sides, official and otherwise, carried back and forth by the packets and their commanders. They carried the mail and the newspapers through the battle for Boston, blockades of New York and British evacuations from former colonial territories. A hunt among government papers and in Post Office archives in London has turned up caches of letters that provide a close-up view of two particular events in packet history that concerned the Boulderson captains: the ransom of the *Prince Adolphus* packet in 1798 and the Falmouth packet seamen's strike of 1810 respectively. Both are explored here.

The broader narrative follows one maritime family over a long period, from the Dutch admiral De Ruyter's raid on the Medway that destroyed Charles II's fleet, to the end of the Napoleonic wars and the final years of the Post Office packet service. These seafarers were ordinary people with particular skills who lived through significant events of their times. This account aims to throw up a few flares over the fractions of the world that they knew.

The Downs and the River

When John Philips Boulderson floats across our field of view for the first time, he is on a merchant vessel in the Downs, off the east coast of Kent. It is the summer of 1744. The *Baltimore* of London, commanded by Jerningham Bigg, is anchored there waiting to head out into the Atlantic, bound for the colonial province of Maryland. John Boulderson is the boatswain, aged not quite 27. In the hold is a consignment of swords, guns, powder and ball purchased by Samuel Hyde on the account of the provincial government. Three days later the *Baltimore* sails down the English Channel in company with five other westbound ships; as far as Portsmouth they are under convoy of the *Suffolk*, a man of war. After that, ship and man pass from our sight again.

On 9 February that year an express letter had reached London from the *Baltimore*, just arrived in the Downs from Maryland, reporting that two days earlier the ship had been detained for several hours off the Lizard by a fleet of 20 French warships. According to Mr Lockhart, the ship's surgeon, 'the Brest Squadron fired thrice sharp into them; and when they asked, why they were insulted on their own Coast by a French Fleet, they received most opprobrious Language'.[4] Although the two countries were not yet formally at war, the previous year an army of British and allied troops led by George II had defeated a French army at Dettingen. At the start of 1744 the French king Louis XV was making plans to invade Britain and install the exiled James Edward Stuart as a compliant James III and VIII. This muscle-flexing by the French fleet off the English coast was followed by reciprocal declarations of war in March.

In May the Admiralty issued a letter of marque to the *Baltimore*, licensing the vessel to go into action against French ships and take prizes. Three weeks later Captain Bigg set sail again with a cargo for Maryland, now armed with 14 carriage guns, eight swivel guns and a gunner from Shadwell. What happened next is not altogether clear.

The ship was listed at Portsmouth on 22 June, but did not arrive in Maryland until five months later. The Atlantic crossing would usually take between five and eight weeks, depending on wind and weather; five months was well outside the span of a single passage, but not time enough for a return and another outward journey.

Unexpectedly, *Lloyd's List* reports that on 21 August 1744 the *Baltimore*, Captain Biggins, sailed from the Downs 'for a Cruize'. The term was used of vessels that were privateering – hunting, seizing and ransoming enemy merchant ships and their cargoes. The *Baltimore* was mentioned twice more the following month as a privateer in the Downs, which would have been the same vessel. Another *Baltimore* was also chasing French and Spanish ships that summer, a navy sloop commanded by Captain Edward Rich, but HM sloop *Baltimore* was then off the coast of Portugal with the merchantmen of the East India fleet.

Was Jerningham Bigg being reckless, to try his luck at privateering while laden with an arms shipment expected in Maryland? He sailed there regularly for the London merchant Samuel Hyde, carrying guns and paper money out, tobacco home. The newly-armed vessel probably sailed outward relatively light, and the initiative had in any case come from Hyde who owned it and licensed another ship at the same time; the *Baltimore* and the *Charles* sailed together. War (as Brecht observed) is a continuation of business by other means, and prize-taking could be far more lucrative than the simple transport of merchandise. Cruising out of the Downs was doubtless how Bigg and his crew spent the missing months, although apparently without success.

The *Baltimore* eventually reached the Chesapeake in November 1744, and the arms were duly accounted for by the Maryland assembly. Some doubts were raised over the precise quantity of gunpowder and shot that had been delivered, because of some missing paperwork.[5] By then, the indigenous nations in the province had given up the fight for their lands, so presumably the provincial government's requirement for swords and guns had become less urgent. News of the treaty with the Six Nations was in England by August.

In April 1745 the *Baltimore* sailed from Maryland for London together with the *Charles* for what would be the last time. We can presume that John Boulderson was still on board, but cannot be sure. The next news of the vessel comes in press reports of a fierce firefight between British and French ships off Ostend at the end of June. The *General Advertiser* in London printed an extract of a letter from Ostend dated 5 July:

> This Morning at One o' Clock, we were alarm'd by a terrible firing of Cannon, which proved to be a Sea-Engagement, close under our Cannon, between his Britannick Majesty's Ships the Bridgwater, Lord George Graham; the Sheerness, Capt. Gordon, and the Ursula Tender, commanded by Lieutenant John Ferguson, who were close engaged with the Royal Privateer, of 28 Guns, the Dutchess de Penthievre, of 26 Guns; and a Dogger, of 18 Guns, all of Dunkirk.[6]

The three French privateers had under their convoy four Atlantic merchant ships and three smaller vessels, all of which they had taken as prizes 'in the North Seas'. The *Baltimore* was one of the merchantmen (the *Charles* got safely home). All four captured merchant ships were armed. Now their crews had been taken prisoner and replaced by French crews.

> The Engagement lasted till Five o'Clock, when the Men of War drove the two great Privateers on Shoar, together with the four large Prizes; and secur'd the two Bremeners; the Dogger Privateer escaped towards Dunkirk. 'Tis impossible to express the Bravery of the three Commanders, who bore the Fire of the three Privateers, as also that of the four Prizes, who are all Ships of Force, and fir'd as much as the Privateers; and so close as Yard-Arm and Yard-Arm [...] The French behaved very bravely, for after Lord George Graham had drove them ashore, they continued firing near half an Hour, before they would strike their Colours.[7]

Charles Brooking (1723–1759), *The Privateer 'Boscawen' Engaging a Fleet of French Ships, 23 May 1745* [National Maritime Museum, Greenwich]. The *Boscawen* was originally a French navy frigate, the *Medée*, which had been captured by a British warship.

The outgunned British navy ships had succeeded in reclaiming the French prizes, but only by running them aground, and themselves also, both sides still firing. All the large ships lay stranded as the tide fell: the two privateers, the four merchantmen and the two British men of war. The correspondent in Ostend continues:

> I have just been down to the Sands, (where they all lye), on board the Royal Privateer who had 40 Men kill'd and 30 wounded; the Dutchess de Penthievre had 30 kill'd and as many wounded; and their Sails so shatter'd that they are Sieves: The Royal's Main-sail is stain'd all over with Blood, and the Blood in great Quantity ran out of her Scupper-Holes. Our Loss is so trifling that it is hardly to be credited.[8]

Most of the ships were later refloated, but the *Baltimore* remained stranded, and only the cargo of tobacco was expected to be saved. The ship was not directly engaged in the triangular slave trade between

England, Africa and the Americas, yet Hyde certainly profited from it since tobacco was produced by the labour of enslaved people. But the war played havoc with Atlantic merchant shipping, which is probably why within a year of that last voyage Hyde was bankrupt. He died not long afterwards.

There was indeed a fear in Britain of invasion that year, but the heroic battle at Ostend described in the newspaper was not purely a matter of national defence. The three navy vessels stood to gain not only the prize money for the capture of the French privateers, but also salvage payments for the rescued British ships. Jerningham Bigg had lost his ship, and can next be found as Samuel Hyde's agent in Annapolis, Maryland, before reappearing a couple of years later on the transatlantic route as master of another vessel. John Boulderson the boatswain, meanwhile, went home to Limehouse and got married, for the second time.

There is no first-hand account of that particular ill-fated trading voyage more than two and a half centuries ago: the people on the *Baltimore* were not chroniclers of their own lives. This momentary glimpse of one individual depends in part on the circumstance that in 1744 Britain went to war with both Spain and France during the convoluted War of the Austrian Succession, and on a piece of regulatory paperwork that puts him there, on that ship. The *Baltimore's* letter of marque from the Admiralty lists the ship's armaments and names the crew.

The movements of the vessel in 1744 can be traced thanks to an early and enterprising news-gathering operation in which the small town of Deal played a prominent part. The town, then as now, had no harbour, just a long shingle beach facing the Downs, 'the great road of England – where sometimes may be seen three or four hundred ships of all sizes at anchor'.[9] The vast open water anchorage or roadstead was protected from enemy fleets in the Channel by the shoals of the Goodwin Sands. William Camden in 1610 remarked on the amphibious nature of the inhabitants of Thanet:

Wenceslaus Hollar (1607–1677), *The Spanish, English and Dutch fleets before Deal, 20 October 1639*, 1640. [Rijksmuseum, Amsterdam]

those especially which dwell by the roads or harboroughs of Margat, Ramsgat and Broadstear. For they are passing industrious, and as if they were *amphibii*, that is, both land-creatures and sea-creatures, get their living both by sea and land, as one would say, with both these elements: they be Fisher-men and Plough men, as well Husband-men as Mariners [...] Furthermore, whereas that otherwhiles there happen shipwrackes here (for they lie full against the shore those most dangerous flats, shallowes, shelves, and sands so much feared of Sailers, which they use to call The Goodwin Sands, The Brakes, The Four-Foots, The Whitdick &.), these men are wont to bestir themselves lustily in recovering both ships, men, and Marchandise endangered.[10]

Deal was an old farming parish lying just below the chalk outcrop, a mile or so inland from Henry VIII's Deal fort. But it encompassed the shoreline between the flanking forts of Walmer and Sandown, whose inhabitants got their living by the sea, one way or another; some had served the Tudor fleet. By the end of the seventeenth century the maritime settlement behind the shingle bank was thriving, and Deal had transformed itself into a charter town whose main business was servicing the fleets of navy and East India ships that lay anchored in the Downs, waiting for orders or a favourable wind. Deal boatmen brought stores to the ships, ferried people between ship and shore, worked as pilots, risked death going to the rescue of

15

those in peril on the Goodwins – and were characterised by Daniel Defoe, notoriously, as barbarous looters who left a thousand sailors to drown in the Great Storm of 1703. The borough threatened to sue.[11] And Dealmen gained a reputation as rapacious smugglers – or, from another viewpoint, free trade men.

The boatmen also brought news ashore. For homecoming London merchant fleets the anchorage in the Downs was often the first point of contact with England, and a chance to send dispatches ahead in the London mails or independently. Since the Restoration, postmasters had been obliged to forward to London the letters brought ashore by ships' masters, and during the eighteenth century the postmaster at Deal received a triple salary: for running the post office, for maintaining a boat and paying boatmen, and for keeping horses and paying postboys to carry the mail as far as Canterbury, where it joined the Dover packet mail for the next stage on the road. Postmasters were usually also innkeepers, and they held the government's monopoly in hiring out horses to travellers on the post roads.[12] The postmaster at Deal in the 1660s and 70s sent weekly lists of ships in the Downs, and any foreign intelligence they brought, to the secretary of state Joseph Williamson and to the Navy Office.[13]

The news operation had its origin in a printed broadsheet first published in the 1690s or earlier by the London coffee house owner Edward Lloyd. It carried news of vital interest to the merchants and underwriters who were his patrons, under two headings: *Ships arrived at, and departed from several ports of England, as I have account of them in London,* and *An account of what English shipping and foreign ships for England, I hear of in foreign ports.* It ran until about 1704, while in 1697 Lloyd launched a newspaper with the snappier title of *Lloyd's News,* which reported foreign events, wars and marine intelligence, but he shut it down again after a few months.

By 1734 the shipping list was back in print under Edward Lloyd's successors. *Lloyd's List* was published twice a week by subscription, carrying systematic lists of the comings and goings at British and foreign ports, together with reports of wrecks and other losses. It out-lived both Lloyd and his coffee house and is still in business today. The surviving early issues, dating from 1741 onwards, make it possible to track some individual eighteenth-century sea passages with considerable precision – including that of the *Baltimore* for Maryland in the summer of 1744.

The voyage of the *Baltimore* began in the river Thames. The ship's owner Samuel Hyde had offices in Rood Lane, a few minutes' walk from the Custom House and legal quays between London Bridge and the Tower. There ships' cargoes were inspected by the Port of London customs men – not always effectively. One London merchant wrote in 1771 to his partner in Maryland:

> I find that the duty on hams is taken off so that, if any of my friends would be so polite as to present me with one now and then, you may assure them there is no danger from the Customs House officers. I likewise have discovered a method to get safe a few bottles of such good old spirit as we used to have. Should any one incline that, I should drink their healths with it. I now and then keep company with Z. Hood Esq, who is very friendly indeed; but, Jonny, you know we have studied the art of smuggling.[14]

The origins of the ship and its crew lay a little way down the river. The fast-growing parishes below the Tower have been described as 'the great engine powering the ascent of the metropolis [...] a site with privileged access to the Thames, an abundance of relatively cheap land and labour, and a refuge from restrictive legislation, which was conveniently close to the financial corridors of the City, and yet remote from the entrances of fashionable residences in the West End.'[15]

A similar view was expressed by the historian John Strype in 1720, although he took city status as the ideal and did not include, in his list of the virtues of Stepney, the legal impunity of operations outside the City's jurisdiction:

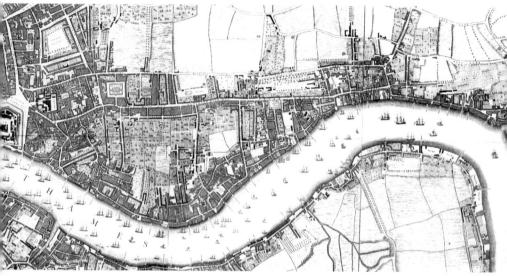

Part of John Rocque's *A plan of the Cities of London and Westminster, and borough of Southwark*, 1746. The Tower is at the left-hand edge and Limekiln Dock at the far right.

Stepney may be esteemed rather a Province than a Parish, especially if we add, that it contains in it both City and Country: For towards the South Parts, where it lies along the River Thames for a great way, by Limehouse, Poplar, and Radcliff, to Wappin, it is furnished with every thing that may intitle it to the Honour (if not of a City, yet) of a great Town; Populousness, Traffick, Commerce, Havens, Shiping, Manufacture, Plenty and Wealth, the Crown of all.[16]

The first John Boulderson

The mariner John Philips Boulderson (1717–1797) was born in one of those crowded riverside hamlets, Ratcliff. Beneath its accretions of wharves and tenements lay a low red cliff which had once been a landmark for early seafarers coming upstream and looking for the gravelly landing place among the marshlands of the old river. Never a parish, perhaps named before there were parishes, the settlement of Ratcliff (written Redecleve or Redclyf in early records) is still there, a reminder that the main road into the city was always the broad looping highway of the Thames. In a coloured print of John Rocque's plan of London, the river looks like a fat blue shiny snake. The settlements clinging like grit to the two flanks of the snake – Wapping, Shadwell, Ratcliff, Limehouse on the north bank, Bermondsey, Rotherhithe, Deptford to the south – grew up on land largely reclaimed from the water, and most of the inhabitants made their living from the river, one way or another.[17]

The origins of John's mother Margaret Philips are uncertain. His father, Joseph Boulderson, was a painter-stainer whose parentage is equally opaque: he seems to materialise in Stepney out of nowhere. Joseph may have been related to a Shadwell mariner of about his own age called John, born to a shipwright in Southwark named Benjamin Bolderston who died a year later, probably at sea. The surname was not a common one, and various spellings were settled upon by a variety of parish clerks.[18] Joseph was certainly connected to Peter Boulderson, a Ratcliff shipwright whose widow Judith would name John Boulderson of Limehouse and his wife Catharine in her will. That opens up the possibility that Joseph Boulderson was born in America to an emigrant family.[19]

In October 1667 a William Bolderson of Canterbury married Mary Terry in Rochester, the old shipbuilding city on the river Medway in Kent. Four months earlier a Dutch fleet had sailed up the Medway and raided the Chatham dockyard where the English navy fleet was laid up for want of money; the Dutch burned most of it and towed away the flagship *Royal Charles*. It was an embarrassing naval catastrophe, but there would have been plenty of work at the dockyard in the urgent rebuilding of the fleet that followed.

William Bolderson's occupation is not recorded and there is no further trace of the couple in Rochester. Back in Canterbury two sons were born, but Mary died soon after undergoing her second childbirth. Later that same year, 1675, William married Joanna Cocke in Canterbury. These two are almost certainly the William and Joanna Boulderson who in 1680 baptised a daughter in the parish of Holy Trinity Minories, within the liberty of the Tower of London.

In the later sixteenth century the parish of Holy Trinity regarded itself as outside the jurisdiction of the English bishops, and drew in radical puritan preachers and their audiences. While that association had faded long before the Bouldersons were there, the parish remained a location for so-called clandestine marriages, conducted outside Church of England regulation. The family was apparently in transit. Their next move was across the Atlantic, to the Massachusetts Bay Colony which had established itself during the 1630s as a puritan stronghold; it was also a place with a substantial shipbuilding industry.

The births of three sons to William and Joanna were recorded by the First Church in Boston; William himself died there in about 1691. At least three of his children were married in Massachusetts and settled there. However the youngest, Peter, born in Boston in 1690, was probably the Ratcliff shipwright of that name who (after a very brief attempt at marriage in Boston) was married at St Dunstan in Stepney in 1727 – a child of the colony who migrated the other way.

As for Joseph, he may have been Peter's elder brother whose birth was recorded in Boston in 1688, but with no forename entered in the register.[20] In truth, these seventeenth-century shipbuilders and mariners were people who belonged to both seaboards of the Atlantic ocean. Some of them could not read or write; their lives and deaths and variable names are recorded on both continents in discontinuous fragments, almost impossible to untangle.

Joseph Boulderson was in Stepney by 1712, when he married Margaret Philips at St Paul Shadwell. He was said to be a painter-stainer. The city livery company of Painter-Stainers at that time encompassed both house-painting and fine art; the court portrait painters Lely and Kneller were members. Later the artists would redefine themselves as having a public purpose beyond that of hired decorators when they founded the Royal Academy, but Joseph Boulderson was undoubtedly an artisan. Yet he makes no appearance in the livery company's records, which adds weight to the case that he was born overseas.

In 1714 he was noted by a parish clerk as living in Ratcliff and working as a 'painter to Shadwell', the adjoining riverside hamlet. He was probably painting ships in one of the small shipyards there, although there could been other work, for example at the church of St Paul in Shadwell with its graveyard full of sea-captains, rebuilt in 1669. In an engraving of the interior it appears to have columns painted as marble. There were a few larger houses there, but there cannot have been many places in that industrial hamlet with a demand for his craft, other than shipyards.

Joseph and Margaret Boulderson's firstborn child, named John, died in infancy, as did the next two. Their fourth child was John Philips Boulderson, born in Ratcliff and baptised at the old mariners' church of St Dunstan Stepney on 8 July 1717, at nine days old. Little is certain about his upbringing and education. His confident handwriting suggests he had a few years' schooling at least, either at the parochial charity school in Shadwell or at one of the Ratcliff charity schools.[21] These took children up to the age of 14, and it is not clear how he spent next the two years before he was apprenticed at 16.

In 1674 a group composed largely of masters of ships set up the Stepney Society with the charitable purpose of paying for orphans and the children of the poor to be apprenticed in the marine trades. In the next century the society's status rose under the patronage of Sir Charles Wager, a Rochester-born rear-admiral who brought more admirals and other magnificos on board. The river trades of lighterman and waterman were included, along with the shipbuilding occupations, and it may well have been under this scheme that in 1733 John Boulderson was apprenticed to a Thames lighterman named Thomas Barnes, at St Katharine's just below the Tower.[22]

The young John was neither an orphan nor truly 'a son of a numerous family, the father of whom is poor and industrious', having only three siblings living (Joseph was probably poor, if not necessarily industrious). But the Society allowed a further option: a master who could not find a suitable orphan or poor boy in order to claim his £5 bounty against the cost of the indenture could take the most promising boy available. The boys were given a book of moral instructions and, to encourage them at the end of the first year, 'a handsome hat and cockade, coat and pair of breeches', plus a dinner and a shilling. If at the end of their term they were found to be still alive and well they got another hat, another dinner and another shilling.[23]

The lightermen belonging to St Katharine's would most probably have been loading and unloading ships moored in the river by the Custom House quay. John Boulderson was indentured for seven years, although he was not formally made free of the company until almost a decade later. However by 1740 he was paying tax at premises on Risby's Ropewalk in Limehouse, which he shared with a mariner named John Smith. Probably he had now moved on from working on the lighters to go to sea on the ships they served.[24] Jerningham Bigg of the *Baltimore* was a near neighbour in Limehouse; he had an address in Green Dragon Alley which was a turning off Risby's Ropewalk, before moving to substantial premises on Fore Street beside Limekiln Dock.

In February 1742 at the age of 24 John married Barbara Copland by licence. In just over a year she was dead of consumption, with no children recorded; she was buried at St Dunstan Stepney. It would be four years before he married again, and he probably spent those

John Boydell (1720–1804), *A view taken near Limehouse Bridge, looking down the Thames*, 1751.
[National Maritime Museum, Greenwich]

years at sea. Captain Bigg with the *Baltimore* crossed the Atlantic between London and Maryland every year from 1741, and before that with another ship. By 1744 John Boulderson was seasoned enough to be employed as boatswain, the foreman in charge of the crew, which on that vessel of 400 tons numbered 34.

John Boulderson's second wife was Katherine Smith. She was probably a sister of his former housemate John Smith, both of them being offspring of a Limehouse mariner named Thomas Smith who owned the house they occupied and the one next to it.[25] John and Katherine were married by licence on 1 June 1746 at St Katharine by the Tower, another of the Tower liberties. Eight years later John Smith married John Boulderson's sister Mary. The Bouldersons were recorded at Risby's Ropewalk until 1756, and during that time Katherine gave birth to two daughters and two sons, all of whom would survive to adulthood, but there is no other trace of the family during those years.[26]

The next time John Boulderson shows up it is in the newspapers, and he is in America. On 18 December 1758 the *New York Gazette* reported the sudden death of Captain Robert Rand on board his vessel the Halifax packet boat, then lying at New York ready to sail for Falmouth. Two days later the *Earl of Halifax* sailed with the mails for England under the command of the master, 'Mr Bolloson'. John Boulderson now had temporary command of a Post Office packet.

Two European powers were in the process of carving out their respective colonies. Boulderson brought with him the news that the French had blown up and abandoned their Fort Duquesne, which was strategically placed at the fork of the Ohio river; the site was now under British command. The indigenous Lenape people (already cheated out of their Delaware territory by the Pennsylvania proprietors) had at first sided with the French in the hope of saving their Ohio lands from further British encroachment, but had now signed a treaty with the British. It was a move that was to prove disastrous for the Lenape, but decisive for the ownership of the Ohio lands.

When John Boulderson brought the *Earl of Halifax* into Falmouth in the middle of January 1759, he 'instantly took Post Horses and came to Town Express', with the news from America.[27] This was well beyond his remit as a packet captain, since the Post Office maintained an established network of post masters and mistresses and their post boys to convey the mails between the ports and London. But Boulderson had his own reasons for travelling urgently to the city, since he also brought the news that Captain Rand was dead.

On 19 January he was commissioned by the General Post Office as 'Commander of the Earl of Halifax Pacquet boat stationed between Falmouth & New York, in the stead of Captaine Rand deceased.'[28] A month later he sailed for New York again, carrying orders from William Pitt the Elder for the restoration of Fort Duquesne.

Captain Boulderson on the packet service

The *Earl of Halifax* was one of four vessels engaged in 1755 for a new mail service from Falmouth to New York. It was a 200-ton ship with six carriage guns, four swivel guns and a crew of 30, then under the command of Captain John Morris. The Post Office contracted with commanders, who provided ship and crew; on the New York service the payment for each return voyage was £700. The Post Office retained packet boat naming rights, hence the array of forgettable aristocrats thus recognised.

As to how John Boulderson from Limehouse came to be in Falmouth, we can make a fair guess. Captain Rand, formerly of Rotherhithe, left Falmouth on his last passage in the *Earl of Halifax* on 31 July 1758, arriving in New York 46 days later, so we know that by then John Boulderson was on the Post Office packet service out of Falmouth, and sufficiently senior to be second in command. It seems likely that he had been returned from Ostend within a few months in a prisoner exchange and, having seen enough of privateering, quickly found work in the service, possibly at Dover which had been a Post Office packet station since the Restoration. Packetmen did not escape the dangers of going into armed conflict, since they were obliged to protect the mails at any cost, but what they did have was legal protection from impressment into the navy, which was a constant threat to seamen whenever they were ashore.

A Dover packet captain named George Balderston was appointed to the Dover–Ostend route in December 1744 with the *Express* packet, having been transferred from the Dover–Calais service which was interrupted by war. He may have been a relative and may have been hiring, although any family connection to John Boulderson remains elusive. Balderston died in October 1755, the same month that the Post Office commissioned the new service between Falmouth and New York.[29] The first of the four packets to sail was the *Earl of Halifax* under Captain Morris, on 13 December 1755.

For eight years after 1755, no children were born to John and Katherine Boulderson. We might guess that John Boulderson worked on the Dover–Ostend packet service from about 1745 and, as an experienced Atlantic sailor, transferred to the Falmouth service on George Balderston's death, while Katherine and their four children remained in Limehouse near her family until he could establish himself in the west. They knew the precariousness of his occupation.

Packet captains were evidently a hardy bunch. In wartime, besides winter storms they ran the risk on each Atlantic crossing of attack by enemy vessels. The packet boats were not supposed to carry freight but they might transport bullion and frequently carried military dispatches, being purpose-built for speed. At about the time Captain Boulderson was setting sail from Falmouth in February 1759 on his first crossing as commander, ahead of him Captain Morris with the *Earl of Leicester* packet reached the anchorage at Sandy Hook below New York. Rather than wait for wind or tide to get up the river, 'Captain Morris with the Mail, came up from the Hook, tho' exposed to the most eminent Danger, in his Boat'.[30]

After an eight-year hiatus Britain was once again formally at war with France, in the conflict known in Britain as the Seven Years' War and in America as the French and Indian War. In January 1761, after firing a salute at Fort George in lower Manhattan to mark George III's accession, the *Earl of Halifax* sailed for Falmouth; in February the packet put into Dartmouth after outrunning six privateers:

> The Halifax packet boat, Captain Balderson, which is arrived at Dartmouth with the mail from New-York, in her passage fell in with four French privateers, but got clear from them after some hours chace. The next day she fell in with two more, one of whom ordered her to bring to, and fired several times at her; but being only within random shot, she received no damage; and tho' they chaced her several hours, yet she happily escaped them. Soon after she met with two more ships, which proved to be English frigates; and having acquainted the Captains with what had happened, they immediately went in pursuit of the privateer.[31]

A view of Fort George with the City of New York from the SW [Library of Congress]. This 1736 view had a long life. Coloured versions were made in the 1760s, and later came one with the flag on the fort painted over to show the American flag. In 1858 it was published in New York as a lithograph, with the British flag restored.

John Boulderson brought with him news of the capture and ransom by a French privateer of another of the New York packets, the *General Wall*, after a long battle in which the packet commander, Walter Lutwidge, was mortally wounded.

That summer his commission was renewed, and his status in the town was cemented when he became an early member of the Falmouth Freemasons' lodge. Its founder was the Post Office packet agent George Bell, who appears to have signed up 20-odd Falmouth packet captains and masters *en masse* sometime before 1770, Boulderson among them. There is (or was), somewhere, an engraved masonic firing glass that formerly belonged to John Boulderson. It brings to mind scenes of brotherly conviviality among the sea-captains – firing glasses were solid little things made to be slammed down on the table in energetic toasts.[32]

The Seven Years' War, fought by Britain against France and Spain, ended in 1763 with the treaty in which Canada was ceded to Britain. That was probably the point at which Captain Boulderson felt secure enough to bring his family to Cornwall. Packet commanders were customarily part-owners of their ships, although it is not clear who owned this one, the first *Earl of Halifax*. In July 1763 the packet made the New York crossing under the command of Henry Jeffery who was probably the master, arriving back in Falmouth in December. He had done so once before when Boulderson was sick, but this time the latter was in London, supervising the building of a new and faster vessel. In January 1764 when he had been a packet commander for five years, he received a new Post Office commission, and on 9 February *The London Evening-Post* reported: 'Monday was launched at Messrs. Collett and Bird's yard, Rotherhithe, a new packet, called the Earl of Hallifax; she was launched with all her rigging standing, a circumstance scarce ever known before.'[33]

John Boulderson was evidently in a hurry. Four weeks later on 8 March the new *Earl of Halifax* arrived in Falmouth, nine days before Captain Jeffery in the older vessel came in with the New York mail, and on 23 April Captain Boulderson set sail in his new packet for New York. The family had probably sailed down together from Limehouse to Falmouth, and Katherine was pregnant. In May their third son was born in Falmouth, and baptised Joseph. Their eldest child Catharine was now almost 16, John was 14 and old enough to go to sea with his father, William was 13 and Mary was nine.

On that first transatlantic crossing the new *Earl of Halifax* brought news from London of the Sugar Act. This was legislation in Parliament to control trade and raise revenue in the colonies, which was to provoke the beginning of the American independence movement under the rallying cry 'no taxation without representation'. And a passenger, Dr William Smith, the provost of the College of Philadelphia, 'arrived in perfect health', noted the *Pennsylvania Gazette*.[34] Packets had six small passenger cabins, each containing one or two narrow bunks. Passengers had to bring their own bedding, and on the homeward passage their provisions also. Carriage of passengers was permitted by the Post Office and provided useful revenue for the ship's captain, if sometimes at the price of giving up his saloon to them. The new vessel seems to have had agreeable accommodation.

The American press reported the arrival of every packet and the British and European news they brought, contained both in the English newspapers and in private letters. Reporters also talked to the packet captains, and Boulderson probably headed straight for the coffee house on arrival in New York. In March 1765 the *Boston Evening-Post* printed this unsettling news:

> Capt. Boulderson [...] reports that the day before he sailed from Falmouth, a letter was received there by a gentleman, from his friend in Plymouth, acquainting him, that several Frenchmen had been just taken up there, as spies, and that on searching their baggage, there was found plans of every sea port town in England, and that it was currently reported, that very party intended to set fire to all the men of war building at Plymouth, &c.[35]

Captain Boulderson's inflammatory intelligence is accounted for, more soberly, by British newspaper reports of a French captain on a passage from Havre to Cork who put in to Plymouth to buy candles, having forgotten to bring any on board. The vessel was detained and the captain, his crew and a passenger were searched by order of the admiral there, 'on suspicious Circumstances, which, on further Examination, appeared frivolous'. Customs returned a quantity of lace and ruffles they had seized from the passenger and the ship was sent on its way.[36]

A year on, and the *Earl of Halifax* reached New York on 17 March 1766 during 'a very hard Gale of wind at East with rain. A perfect storm'. The man recording the extreme New York weather was a

British army engineer named John Montresor, who noted Captain Boulderson's battle with the elements and also the significant arrival of a navy passenger.

> Notwithstanding, this day arrived the Halifax Packet from Falmouth, she struck on the East Bank (in coming up from Sandy Hook) 8 times and sprung a leak [...] The Captain of the Packet, in 22 voyages to this Port from England never met with once, so tempestuous as this last. On his arrival cut, off from the vessel's masts and rigging over 20 Tons of Ice; in her came Captain Conner to command the Coventry in the room of Captain Kennedy superceeded by order of His Majesty for refusing to take charge of the Stamps of this Province on board his Ship from Lieut. Govr. Colden.[37]

Kennedy's difficulty related to a piece of legislation yet more contentious than the Sugar Act: the Stamp Act of 1765, which imposed a tax on colonial paperwork, including port clearance of merchant vessels. It was fiercely resisted, and further stiffened revolutionary resolve. By the time Kennedy left New York on the *Earl of Halifax* two weeks after Conner's arrival, the Act had already been hastily repealed, but the political damage was done.

For two years from March 1767 the *Earl of Halifax* was commanded by Henry Jeffery. Boulderson retained the Post Office contract, but he was now 50 years old, with a family of six children aged from 19 down to newborn. John Flavel, the seventeenth-century Dartmouth preacher quoted above in the introduction, had himself narrowly escaped shipwreck in a storm off Portland and knew what would resonate with his flock. 'To see Men that have spent so many Years upon the Seas (where your Lives have continually hung in suspense before you) attain to your Years [...] Oh, what cause have you to adore your great Preserver!'[38]

In truth the stoical John Boulderson was more likely concerned with practical matters. On the day he came ashore in February 1767 his seafaring eldest son John turned 17, and in November his daughter Catharine married a Falmouth merchant by the name of Samuel

Groube. The following year his son William was apprenticed to a Falmouth upholsterer. The Bouldersons are said to have lived in Mulberry Square, where the Custom House then stood.[39] It was probably about that time that John Boulderson the elder started work on building a substantial granite house in the country for his retirement. Boswarren (now Bosvarren House) still stands in the parish of Constantine, about five miles south-west of Falmouth.

Detail with seamen going aloft, from *A British Man of War Firing a Salute*, *c.* 1750–59, by Charles Brooking (1723–1759). [Tate Britain]

The second Captain Boulderson

When the *Earl of Halifax* sailed for New York in April 1769 it was under the command of Captain Boulderson again. This was most probably the son. John Boulderson II (1750–1831) was just 19 years old but would have been sailing under his father for several years. Certainly by the summer of 1771 the younger Boulderson was in command of the packet; that information comes from the merchant and slave-trader Henry Laurens, then on a journey from South Carolina to England. He wrote from New York on 4 September: 'I arrived in this City three days ago, and am to embark to morrow on board the E of Halifax Packet, Capt. Bolderson', and later referred to him as the younger Boulderson. Once on board he observed: 'We are in a fine Vessel just in good Ballast, and the Captain except swearing a little too much, seems to be just what we would wish him.'[40] After a passage of 29 days, Laurens wrote from Falmouth to a Quaker merchant in Philadelphia whose son had travelled with him:

> Capt. Boulderson commander of the Packet introduced us early to an Acquaintance with his Father, and our Friend Samuel Groube. These Gentlemen paid us the Compliment of a formal Visit and unlimited offers of Service. Yesterday we dined with Mr Groube, and are under a Promise if we tarry 'till Noon, to eat Fish at the elder Capt. Boulderson's, but for divers good Reasons I intend to set out for Bristol before dinner Time.[41]

Samuel Groube had been trying to get business from Laurens for some time, and was hoping for a deal to import South Carolina rice at Falmouth rather than Laurens's usual arrangements with a merchant at Cowes. Laurens agreed to a trial but they subsequently fell out, apparently over Groube's expectation of special treatment.[42] Laurens paid £100 for the passage to Falmouth: for himself, his two sons, a friend's son and a fifth person, his servant Scipio, who also served as a companion to his sons. The enslaved Scipio was an independent-minded individual who now insisted on being called Robert (perhaps his own name, or perhaps a new persona). When Laurens returned to America in 1774 Robert did not go with him; after a reportedly bigamous marriage and a jail sentence for the theft of a ham, he vanishes from our sight somewhere in London and appears lost to history.[43]

Falmouth was known for its excellent fish. Laurens noted in the Falmouth letter that they had feasted on fish three times a day, listing eight varieties; he had clearly had enough. The people on the packets might also eat fresh fish *en voyage*. 'Little winds & Calms and what we had as unfavourable as could be, with a tumbling Sea & small thick cold Rain [...] got the Lines out in hopes of taking some Mackarel but our Bait was not tempting enough', wrote the packet Captain Edward Lawrance on a passage from Falmouth to Madeira in the summer of 1776. At Madeira they tried, and failed, to land a Devil Fish, which he described as like a skate but 10 feet long. He added that his sailors bought some tons of onions there very cheap, to sell on at their next port of call in the West Indies: 'every Part of the Vessel is full of them, she stinks so strong of them, that if any People were two or three Leagues to Leeward of us they might easily smell us out'.[44]

Fish dinners may have been a Boulderson speciality, if not to Laurens's patrician taste. The menu reappears a decade later in the next generation. Another acquaintance of the Bouldersons was a mariner from St Ives named Samuel Kelly, who was the same age as the younger John Boulderson's brother Joseph and attended the grammar school in Helston with him.

Kelly began his seagoing career as a boy on the packets, usually as a cabin steward. When he was 18 and second mate on the *Grenville* packet, he found himself temporarily under Joseph Boulderson's command. In the summer of 1782 while they were in Falmouth harbour, Joseph (or possibly his older brother John) organised a river excursion to Mylor with friends, in two boats. Kelly was in the crew of the smaller one, which was equipped with a seine net to catch fish for a dinner party. He was embarrassed to find that the company included a gentleman and three ladies he had known at Helston.

> This discovery was very mortifying to me, for though I was dressed clean and decent, I was now only an associate of vulgar seamen [...] a message was sent from Captain B. to me, demanding my presence to fry some of the fish. But whether this was by way of insult, or from knowing I understood the business, I am at a loss to determine. For he must have been aware that the ladies had formerly known me. However, I went to the house and informed a person that I saw there that it was my opinion women were better acquainted with cookery than myself, and that I did not like to undertake to cook for ladies.[45]

In December 1772 John Boulderson the elder retired formally from the packet service and his son John was commissioned in his place. He was to enjoy 25 years of prosperous retirement with his wife at Boswarren (now Bosvarren), the owner of freehold and copyhold property as well as his quarter share in the *Earl of Halifax*.

Bosvarren House in 2003

The American revolutionary war

The elder Boulderson's former sailing-master Henry Jeffery was now in command of another Falmouth to New York packet, the *Lord Hyde* (there were usually five of them). Following a year or so of unremarkable crossings, when Captain Jeffery sailed to New York in the summer of 1775 he became entangled in the outbreak of the revolutionary war, not as a combatant but as an informant. When he came ashore in the city on 17 June 1775 he was called before the New York provincial Congress for questioning.[46] The Congress reported the same day to the Continental Congress in Philadelphia that Captain Jeffery of the *Lord Hyde* had relayed to them movements of British ships.

> We are this day informed by *Mr. Jeffrey*, of the *Lord Hyde* packet-boat, that the *Mercury* ship-of-war was cruising off our coast, and is now at *Sandy-Hook*, to order the transports from *Ireland* with Troops destined to this City, to proceed immediately to *Boston*; and did on *Tuesday* last, about thirty leagues to the southeast of *Sandy-Hook* deliver those orders to the *Old Spy*, man-of-war, (now a transport with a part of the Forty-Fourth Regiment on board,) who immediately altered her course. Captain *Jeffery* told us he had this information both from the officers of the troops on board of the *Spy*, and from some of the officers of the *Mercury* man-of-war. From this information, we are induced to conclude that some capital stroke is meditated against our brethren of the *Massachusetts-Bay*. We therefore, gentlemen, think it our duty to despatch this information to you, that it may be known to the Continental Congress.[47]

News of the battles at Lexington and Concord on 19 April had not reached England when Captain Jeffery sailed from Falmouth on 11 May, but his betrayal of military intelligence looks like something other than ignorance. By the time he went ashore in New York five weeks later he can have been in no doubt that the two countries were at war. It was reported that the mail brought over on the *Lord Hyde* had been put on board a man of war at Sandy Hook, below New York;

the packet captain probably carried it on board the *Mercury* frigate himself.[48] A week later came this American press report:

> New-York, June 29. Whereas it has been reported, that goods were imported in the packet to this place contrary to the association of the Continental Congress. — The Committee having made proper inquiry, do certify to the public, that Henry Jeffreys, commander of the Lord Hyde Packet, has given full satisfaction, that no goods have been imported in his vessel this voyage, either on his own account, or the account of any other person whatever.[49]

Captain Jeffery was presumably induced to talk to secure the release of himself and his ship. He must have kept quiet afterwards about his encounter with the Congress, since there appears to be no record of it in the press on either side of the Atlantic, nor of any disciplinary action against him after he reached Falmouth in September. Who knows which cause he favoured? Perhaps it was simply his own. By contrast, when the New York Congress called in a Captain Thompson from Cork three days before they saw Jeffery, having heard he had news of troop transports heading for New York, they noted Thompson's remark that 'the people of Ireland in general are well affected to the Americans, and are averse to the Americans being taxed by the Parliament of Great Britain'.[50]

The way that news of the outbreak of the Revolution first reached England is itself something of a story. The British commander, General Gage, sent his dispatches on 24 April by a hired merchant ship, but the *Sukey* was not first across with the news. The Massachusetts provincial Congress, keen to get their version of events to London first, sent the *Quero*, a fast schooner owned by a Congress member, Richard Derby, and commanded by his brother John.

Captain Derby was told to land somewhere in Ireland or Scotland to avoid discovery, and continue from there. He sailed in ballast from Salem on 28 April. Sensibly enough he ignored instructions and proceeded to the Isle of Wight, crossed to Southampton and hired a

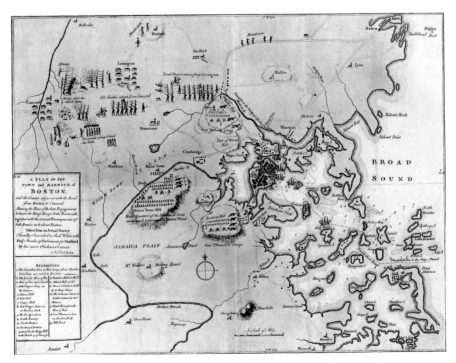

A plan of the town and harbour of Boston and the country adjacent with the road from Boston to Concord, shewing the place of the late engagement between the King's troops & the provincials, London, 29 July 1775 [Library of Congress]. A broken line threading its way through the islands at lower right indicates the ship channel to the city.

post-chaise to London. He arrived in the city late on 28 May, bringing a letter addressed to Benjamin Franklin, sworn depositions of fact and copies of the *Essex Gazette,* a Salem newspaper. Within a couple of days the sensational news had travelled around the country. Gage's dispatches reached London on 10 June, confirming the story; the only point at issue was who had fired first. Meanwhile the *Quero*'s sailing-master brought the schooner round to Falmouth, arriving on 3 June. Derby rejoined his vessel there to return to Salem and make his report to George Washington and the Continental Congress.[51]

The comings and goings of John Boulderson the younger during that fevered summer were likewise recorded in the British and
the American press. In 1775 the *Oxford Journal* reported: 'London,
August 3. Last night the dispatches from the Secretary of State's
Office, &c. were made up, and sent to the General Post Office, and
from thence sent off express to Falmouth, to be put on board the
Hallifax Packet Boat, Boulderson, with orders to sail for New-York
the first fair wind.'[52]

The same issue of the *Oxford Journal* led with news of a battle at
Bunker's Hill, which overlooked Boston. The British had defeated
the new Continental Army but taken severe losses. The urgent dispatches from Lord Dartmouth, the secretary of state for the colonies,
included a notably unhelpful memo to Sir Guy Carleton, governor of
the province of Quebec, expressing the hope that there would be an
army of 20,000 in North America 'next spring', along with orders to
the British commander at the place later known as Bunker Hill, General Thomas Gage, to hand over to General William Howe and return
to England.[53]

On 28 September at the height of this smouldering tension the
Earl of Halifax anchored in New York harbour. On 19 October the
British governor of New York, William Tryon, wrote to the mayor of
New York (a native New Yorker) from on board Boulderson's vessel.
Tryon had installed himself there for his own safety, after learning
that the Continental Congress planned to have him arrested.

> On board the Halifax Packet, October 19, 1775.
> Sir : Finding your letter of yesterday insufficient for that security I
> requested from the Corporation and citizens, and objectionable for
> the mode in which you obtained the sense of the inhabitants, my duty
> directed me, for the present instant, to remove on board this ship,
> where I shall be ready to do such business of the Country as the
> situation of the times will permit.[54]

Tryon remained there for some time before transferring on 30
October to set up his office on the merchant ship *Duchess of Gordon*

which lay under the protection of a British warship – no doubt to the relief of Captain Boulderson who would have been obliged to give up his saloon to his guest. 'This measure though expensive was necessary as I could not have kept up any communication with the Country had I gone on board the Asia Man of War, Whereas in my present situation the Friends of Government freely come to me', was Tryon's justification to the secretary of state.[55] There he continued to receive intelligence from his informers, including this:

> Secret Intelligence. Miss Watson Milliner from Philadelphia going to England in the Hallifax Packet is charged with one letter or dispatch, from the Continental Congress, another from the Revd. Docr. Rogers of the City of N. York and others, and also with an Annonymous letter or Packet.
> Note Miss Watson dresses in a Riding Habit or dress[56]

Tryon sent this message across to Boulderson on the *Earl of Halifax* with a covering letter instructing him not to let the courier leave his vessel on their arrival in England:

> Sir / Having received the inclosed information that Miss Watson, with certain letters is going passenger in the Hallifax Packet, you will be carefull not to suffer neither her person nor her Baggage to leave your ship until you have made known to a Magistrate at Falmouth, (or where you first land in England) the within intelligence, and proper search has been made, for the dispatches She carries believed to contain matters of a Treasonable nature.[57]

Captain Boulderson now began the four-week voyage home, living at close quarters with his passengers on the small vessel, all the while knowing he would hand over Miss Watson on arrival. Perhaps he told her. When they reached Falmouth on 14 December he gave Tryon's letter to the mayor, who as it happened was his brother-in-law Samuel Groube. The latter called in the collector of customs and the postmaster, who seized the letters they found in Miss Watson's baggage. Groube took a statement on oath from his brother-in-law

Boulderson, who certified the prisoner's identity and the authenticity of the documents; Boulderson himself wrote to Anthony Todd, secretary of the Post Office, with information as to ships fitted out by the rebels at Philadelphia, and enclosed a copy of a motion of General Washington's, sent to the different committees but thought too bad to be printed.[58]

Groube presumably searched Miss Watson's person at that point, since the anonymous letter was not discovered until he had her in custody. He seems also to have found out, possibly from Boulderson, that the writer was 'Dr B R of Philada'. That was Dr Benjamin Rush, a Philadelphia physician and social reformer who would later be a signatory to the Declaration of Independence. In the letter Rush recommended Miss Watson to a former fellow-student now practising in England, thanked him for his news which was often published in the American press, and gave a buoyant account of political and military developments on the revolutionary side.[59]

Groube sent her on her way and sent the seized documents to the secretary of state, adding to his account of the operation: 'I hope that our conduct in this affair will meet with your Lordship's approbation and that in future we shou'd be glad of your Lordship's directions how to act upon any Similar occasion and particular against such person or persons on whom such letters are found secreted.'[60] As ever, he was hoping for personal advantage or preferment (he was to be disappointed again), but he may also have borne a personal grudge. He would have been aware that Henry Laurens, the man who had rebuffed him four years earlier, was now a revolutionary politician and president of the South Carolina Congress.

As for the Philadelphia milliner dressed in a riding habit, she was a Scotswoman named Margaret (or Peggy) Watson. Further work for the rebels as a secret courier presumably now being out of the question, she went back to Scotland, got married, and after American independence returned there and settled in Pittsburgh with her husband, Hugh Ross, who built a distillery. Captain Boulderson seems

Archibald Robertson, *No 5 of the Circle of Boston, 7 March 1776* [New York Public Library].
Detail from one of five views sketched from fortifications overlooking the city on 4 January
1776, finished later. Boston is seen behind Charlestown, and at right is Bunker's Hill.
Robertson was a British lieutenant of engineers.

to have remained ashore for the next six months, probably while the
Earl of Halifax was refitted and rearmed; on the next crossing the
packet would be obliged to run a blockade of American privateers.
He subsequently proved to be a combative individual.

As John Boulderson was sailing back to Falmouth towards the end
of 1775, Henry Jeffery was heading the other way in the *Lord Hyde*.
The British post office in New York ceased operation at the end of the
year, supplanted by Benjamin Franklin's new Constitutional Post,
and on 3 January 1776 Captain Jeffery arrived at Boston, which was
under siege by Washington's Continental army on the landward side
northwest of Charlestown, while the harbour was still controlled by
the British navy. From there he wrote to Todd to explain why he was
not at Quebec:

> After a very troublesome passage I arrived in the Gulf of St Lawrance on
> the 22d of November where I continued beating and endeavouring to
> enter the River 'till the 9th of December having almost the whole time
> continual Snow Storms with very heavy Gales of Wind and excessive
> bad weather, the Vessel for the general part covered with Ice to such a
> degree that it was with the utmost difficulty I could work her, many of
> my Men being Frost bitten and the rest so benumbed with the cold, that
> nothing but force could make them stand the Deck.[61]

On 31 January, he wrote to Todd again with intelligence that an attack on Boston harbour was expected, and also that privateers had taken four ships; he was still detained there and could not say when he would sail. In wartime the packets came under military command and he was being held for dispatches.[62]

The *Lord Hyde* was the next packet to leave Boston with the mails, but did not sail for Falmouth until the British army under General Howe evacuated Boston by sea on 17 March, bound for Halifax. Jeffery parted company with the convoy off Nantucket on 25 March. The *Lord Hyde* was carrying upwards of 300 letters, and among the passengers were the families of the Massachusetts chief justice and the governor; the latter was already in London. There were seven children on board.[63] Captain Jeffery may have decided to write to Todd to cover his back; however it was usual for packet commanders to pass on wartime intelligence and there is no evidence that his loyalty was ever doubted by the British.

The colonial chief justice Peter Oliver followed his family back to England from Halifax on the *Harriot* packet. His diary provides a graphic narrative of icebergs and a fog-bank off Newfoundland, sea-sickness, followed by an idyllic early-morning view of Falmouth as he saw it in the summer of 1776: 'a populous town, a fine harbour, handsome well-built keys, stone and brick buildings, high and well cultivated lands all in verdure, and arranged like gardens with their allotments separated by hedges.'[64]

This picture of contented prosperity echoes the impression the town made upon someone who saw it two decades earlier, the African Olaudah Equiano. Born possibly in Guinea, Equiano was purchased in Virginia as a frightened child slave by Captain Pascal of the merchantman *Industrious Bee*. He was about 11 years old when the ship reached Falmouth after a passage of 13 weeks from Virginia. 'I was very much struck with the buildings and the pavement of the streets in Falmouth', he wrote in his memoir. And he was bewildered when he saw snow that had fallen on the deck; he thought it must be salt.[65]

Jan Brandes (1750–1808), *De Strand Straat te Falmouth, 9 June 1778* [*Album van Jan Brandes*, vol. 2, Rijksmuseum, Amsterdam]. Brandes was a Dutch Lutheran pastor on a passage to Batavia who spent a few days ashore in Falmouth. He notes that this view is from the gallery above the front door of the King's Arms.

Captain Boulderson sailed again from Falmouth with the *Earl of Halifax* in June 1776; as the members of the Continental Congress in Philadelphia were signing the Declaration of Independence he was somewhere on the Atlantic. Washington's regiments had marched 200-odd miles south to New York, while on 2 July General Howe began to assemble an army on Staten Island for an assault on the city. The *Earl of Halifax* arrived there on 11 August, after successfully fighting off a privateer in a battle that lasted an hour and a half, it was reported.

> Staten Island, Aug. 17, 1776. Colonel Guy Johnson is arrived here from England; on the Passage in the Halifax Packet, a privateer engaged her, but after Capt. Boulderson had gallantly defended his Ship three Glasses, the Adventurer ended the Contest by a Retreat.[66]

43

By 27 September when Boulderson sailed again for England, the British army and navy forces under General Howe and his brother, the admiral Lord Richard Howe, had completed their capture of the city from Washington (a hollow victory as it turned out, since Washington evaded capture and saved his army). Thus the indomitable Captain Boulderson was a witness to a crucial battle in the Revolutionary war, and also to the devastating fire that destroyed a part of New York very soon afterwards. He left no account of what he saw, and he was not first home with the news, but he did have on board the *Earl of Halifax* an aide dispatched by General Howe to deliver his reports of the capture of New York and of the fire to the colonial secretary in London.[67]

Relations between the Post Office and British military powers were prickly. 'Every Thing is kept an impenetrable Secret here' was the complaint of the postmaster at Quebec, who in May 1777 could offer Todd in London no solid intelligence on British troop movements.[68] Eighteen months later, Todd at the General Post Office in Lombard Street sent over a furious letter to the under-secretary of state for the American department in Whitehall, requesting that an order be sent out that night to the British military commander at New York, who was commandeering the incoming mails.

> As the Mails for New York and the West Indies are to be made up
> this Evening, there will not be time for a Letter from The Postmaster
> General to My Lord George Germain, to request his Lordship would
> have the Goodness to write by this Opportunity to the Commander
> in Chief at New York, not to detain the packet Boats longer than may
> absolutely be necessary, particularly at this time when the Service has
> been so greatly deranged by the Capture of several of them [...] a great
> Confusion has been occasioned in the Correspondence with New York
> by the Mail, being carried to and opened by the Commander in Chief,
> as great part of the Letters are never delivered and very little postage
> collected, so that our Accounts from the Deputy Postmaster General
> are very defective and confused, which might easily be remedied if the

Mails were delivered as they certainly ought to the Deputy General who would of course take care to distribute all Letters and Dispatches for the Commanders in Chief in the first place, and to the Officers and Army in general, with the utmost Expedition.[69]

John Boulderson the younger made two more crossings to New York, then transferred with the *Earl of Halifax* to the West Indies route in the summer of 1777. In February 1778, when the packet was in Falmouth and on the point of sailing for the Caribbean for the second time, the packet agent Stephen Bell (son of George) wrote to Anthony Todd with alarming news about shipworm.

> This Morning Captn Boulderson came to my office, & informed me, that after his Packet Boat, the Halifax, was removed to the moorings, & every minute Article put on Board, she became so leaky, as to make three feet of water in 12 Hours, that he was greatly alarmed, had rehauled her on Shore & desired I would look at her bottom, & endeavour to investigate the cause of the Leak. As soon as the Water had left her, I requested the most intelligent & scientific People in that branch of Business, in this place to attend me, when we found on taking the Tallow from her bottom, that the Worms had made a rapid Progress in, and a dreadful havock on it, and it was the unanimo[u]s Opinion of the Company, that there would be imminent Danger in her proceeding to Sea without being sheathed.[70]

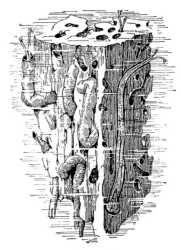

It seems extraordinary that a hull so disastrously riddled with holes should not have been spotted when the vessel was hauled out to be cleaned after the previous voyage, and Bell thought so. But he accepted the assurances of the captain and the shipwright:

Teredo navalis

45

that they had nicely inspected it, & were deceived by the Ta[r] & stuff being heated in burning the bottom, which filled up, & rendered these Wormholes imperceptible that became visible by a second burning, and scraping the bottom perfectly clean this day. As her Planks in the bottom are so greatly damaged, & the Worms have made innumerable Cavities through them, even into the Timbers, Copper Sheathing cannot be made use of, & consequently Fir Sheathing is the only Remedy [...] I cannot avoid saying, that a similar Deception might, & may happen to any other Person, & that Capt Boulderson feels greatly for it.[71]

Captain Boulderson sent a terse and not noticeably apologetic letter to Todd by the same post, informing him that 'we shall proceed to sheath her with Fir, which our Builder promises to compleat in 6 Weeks'. The packet sailed for Jamaica by way of Madeira a little under eight weeks later.[72]

When John Boulderson arrived back in Falmouth from Jamaica for the second time the following summer, his wife-to-be was most probably also on board. Eleven days later, on 14 September 1778, he was married in Falmouth to Mary Williams. She is said to have been from St Helena. That could mean she was from the island in the South Atlantic, which then belonged to the East India Company and was a strategic port of call on the passage from the East Indies; but John Boulderson II did not sail so far south. The route established by the Post Office in 1769 for the West Indies packets was between Jamaica, Pensacola in Florida and Charleston in South Carolina.

Charleston, and the smaller town of Beaufort a little way down the coast, had deep-water anchorages serving the rice and indigo plantations whose output was destined for England (and whose workers were, of course, enslaved people). The flat sea-island country around Beaufort had a further asset: forests of cypress, pine and live or evergreen oak. The dense timber of live oak was resistant to rot, making it particularly well suited for shipbuilding, and its branching growth provided curved timbers for making the knee braces that supported decks. The Beaufort shipwrights also undertook repairs, and if work

were needed on the *Earl of Halifax* after the westward passage, that is most probably where it would have been done. The old parish in which Beaufort lay was named St Helena.

Mary Williams resists identification, although the name Williams appears variously in St Helena parish records of the time, most often in reference to a merchant and attorney named Robert Williams who had a hand in much local business. John Boulderson had already encountered the South Carolina merchant Henry Laurens, and probably others who took passage on the New York packets. But Laurens at least was now a leading American patriot. A British amphibious assault on Charleston in the summer of 1776 was a failure, and in 1777 the South Carolina legislature imposed an oath of allegiance to the new government, which resulted in an exodus of British loyalists, some of them now in financial difficulty. The packets could no longer call at Charleston, but Captain Boulderson is known to have sailed to Jamaica late in 1777, and then again the next summer. It was at the end of the latter voyage that he married Mary Williams. She probably belonged to a loyalist family in South Carolina, and left there by way of the West Indies during the revolutionary war.[73]

Mary Boulderson gave birth to their first child on 15 June 1779 while her husband was somewhere across the Atlantic on the West Indies route. The child was named John after his father and grandfather, but not baptised until his father got home. That was much later than Mary might have hoped, in December. It had been noted that summer that the *Earl of Halifax* was fir-sheathed rather than with copper; since 1775 the packet commanders had been expected to copper-sheath their vessels for speed, since they sailed out of convoy and were under orders to attempt to outsail any attacker. But still, Boulderson's ship 'was reckoned a very prime sailer', according to a newspaper report in November that the *Earl of Halifax* had not been heard of since leaving Jamaica on 12 July.[74]

Five days later further news reached London. On 20 August 1779 the packet had been taken by an American privateer, the *General Starke*, and carried into Salem in Massachusetts.[75] Next came news that the *Earl of Halifax* had been retaken by a British navy cruiser and carried into New York, but that turned out to be untrue, and by October the Post Office knew the vessel was lost to the Americans. On 1 December details came in from New York that the packet had fought for two and a half hours, and four of the crew were dead.

> The Halifax packet-boat, Captain John Boulderson, with the West-India mail, was taken near the coast of England by the General Stark privateer of 22 six and nine pounders; the engagement lasted five glasses, the Halifax had four men killed, and six or seven wounded, one of the latter James Dashwood, Esq; slightly in the heel. They are carried into Salem.[76]

Finally, in the *Derby Mercury*:

Extract of a Letter from Falmouth, dated December 13. The Captains, Officers, Crews, and some of the Passengers of the Halifax Packet-Boat, from Jamaica, and the Sandwich from New-York, taken by the Rebels, arrived Yesterday at Mountsbay from Boston, after a Passage of 30 Days, and late last Night Captains Hill and Bolderson arrived here. We understand they are not exchanged, but are under Promise to deliver an equal Number of Prisoners to the American Agents in France.[77]

The people from the two packets returned on a vessel hired at Boston. The objective of privateers was to capture vessels and their cargoes with as little damage to the prize as possible; with luck they might also get their hands on their enemy's mail and military dispatches. Post Office packet boats had orders to place the mail in a weighted bag hung over the side of the vessel when armed engagement was expected, and cut it loose to sink if they were about to be boarded.

The packet captains were under orders to fight to the last for their vessels, and sometimes they were aided by their passengers; these were desperate battles. However, once possession was achieved those on board were transferred as prisoners to the privateer, a skeleton crew was put into the captured vessel to bring it in, and there was an internationally-recognised system for the exchange and return of captured crews to their home ports. Under those rules, Captain Boulderson was to remain on parole until May 1781, during which time he was bound by a mutual obligation (as if imprisoned) not to go to sea. The Post Office paid him £4,050 compensation for the loss of his vessel, and in May 1781 a new, 157-ton, copper-sheathed *Earl of Halifax* left the Thames for Falmouth, the third packet of that name.

That same month, evidently concluding that superior force was wanted as well as speed, Boulderson obtained a letter of marque from the Admiralty against the French. The Post Office officially disapproved of the practice, but he was not the only packet captain to do it. From it we find that John Boulderson and his father were joint owners of the new vessel, and also a description:

of the burthen of 160 Tons square sterned Figure Head and has two Masts that the said John Boulderson goeth Comr. of her that She is Mounted with 6 Carriage Guns Carrying Shot of 6 Pounds Weight and 20 Swivel Guns is Navygated with 60 Men has 60 Small Arms 60 Cutlasses 10 Barrels of Powder 30 Rounds of Great Shot and about 500 Weight of Small Shot that the said Ship is Victualled for 6 Months has 2 Suits of Sails 3 Anchors 3 Cables and about 1000 Weight of Spare Cordage.[78]

In June the third *Earl of Halifax* sailed on the New York route, arriving home in November. The packet's next departure from Falmouth was in March 1782 for Madeira and Charleston (at that point under British occupation), and Boulderson's younger brother Joseph was sailing-master. At Charleston Samuel Kelly appears on the scene. He was cabin boy on the *Grenville* packet, which was sailing the same route and had been captured by an American privateer, then retaken by a British navy sloop and sent in to Charleston, where the *Earl of Halifax* was already in port. Although the privateer had taken off most of the crew, Kelly remained and was still on board when in April some of the *Earl of Halifax*'s crew were transferred to bring the *Grenville* home. Kelly provides an eyewitness account of the capture by the privateer:

> On the 15th March we had lightning from all quarters, and saw a large waterspout at a distance. On the 18th a ship chased us, and on the 19th about eleven at night she drew very near. Called all hands to quarters, after which the ship hailed us, and informed us she was an English cruiser, ordering at the same time our boats to be sent on board, which was attended to, and the boat returned with strange armed men, instead of our boat's crew. On their coming on deck, they informed our captain that the ship's name was the *Trumball* (I believe), an American frigate, on which our captain gave the signal for our mail to be sunk, and surrendered the ship without any further ceremony.[79]

The American vessel turned out to be the *Franklin* of Salem, scarcely better armed than the *Grenville*, and Kelly took the view that

Francis Holman (1729-1784), *A Small Shipyard on the Thames*, 1774-84 [National Maritime Museum, Greenwich]. This is thought to depict a Rotherhithe yard. The third *Earl of Halifax* may, like the second, have been built at Quallet and Bird's at Rotherhithe. The mastless vessel on the slipway looks about the size of a Post Office packet.

they could have beaten her off if not taken her, had their commander been a man of spirit. He catalogues a Keystone Cops journey towards Boston with an incompetent crew: 'I exerted myself to the utmost aloft, and on laying out on the main-top sail-yard to furl the sail, for want of active assistance, I was a considerable time wrapped up on the yard in the sail [...] on my going down into the cabin, found the water had got in there, and a quantity of cheese being loose, and the wet getting to them, made them so slippery that they were running from side to side almost every roll'. The American crew cut up the cheese and fried it for their dinner, while Kelly discovered two boxes of preserved citron which he kept for himself.[80]

The *Grenville* returned to Falmouth under the command of Joseph Boulderson, 'Captain Lofty' according to Kelly, who was now sailing

51

as second mate but still had to work aloft. He vents his grievances against the entitled Bouldersons:

> This captain was about two years older than myself, and his father (an old captain) lived next door to my father in Falmouth, and before we went to sea, was my intimate acquaintance and boon companion; but at home, after I had begun to sail in the packets (his brother having pushed him forward, and I having no friend) he began to show his superiority by slighting and totally withdrawing himself from my society [...] My station at sea was, as usual, in the main-top, where I experienced much hectoring and uncivil language from the captain below, who had evidently forgotten himself, and never once during the passage home, gave me a bit of fresh victuals, or even treated me with more civility than the crew experienced from him, though he was even rioting on poultry, hogs, etc.[81]

The *Grenville* was subsequently renamed and sailed on the same service under a different captain. It was after that voyage under Joseph Boulderson that Kelly's fish-frying humiliation took place, and he left the packet service soon afterwards. While he undoubtedly bore a festering grudge against the Bouldersons, he may have had a point where Joseph Boulderson in particular was concerned, whose later career tends to bring to mind a pompous and not altogether like-able individual. More about him later.

At war with France, again

In September 1783 the ending of British rule in what was now the United States of America was sealed with the Treaty of Paris, and Britain signed peace treaties with the France and Spain; a treaty with the Dutch Republic was signed eight months later. For the next decade the *Earl of Halifax* continued on the West Indies and New York routes without evident incident, until the next outbreak of hostilities.

Mary Boulderson gave birth to six more children. She died at the age of 38 in January 1792, a little over a year after the youngest child was born and when the eldest, John, was 12. The cause of her death is not known. At least four children lived to adulthood, and John the widower would outlive Mary by nearly 40 years, but he does not seem to have remarried. The care of his children presumably fell to their grandparents at Boswarren or their aunts and uncles in Falmouth, at least while their father continued on the Atlantic service.

In March 1794 Captain Boulderson brought the news home from Jamaica of the impending British invasion of Martinique, early in the French revolutionary war. It was his final Atlantic crossing, since he had now achieved seniority in the service and with it the privilege of transferring to the easier and more profitable Falmouth to Lisbon station. He sailed that route once only with the *Earl of Halifax*; the vessel was then returned to the transatlantic service under a different captain because it was copper-bottomed, while Boulderson hired the *Jane*, a temporary packet, for the Lisbon service. He put another captain on the *Jane* while he stayed ashore to supervise the construction of a new packet. This one was built at a local yard named Little Falmouth, which lay on the opposite bank of the Penryn river above Flushing and was run by the Symons family of shipwrights.

In February 1797 John Boulderson II was commissioned on the Lisbon service with his new vessel, the 180-ton *Prince Adolphus*, and sailed from Falmouth for Lisbon a month later. About a week after that his 17-year-old son, the third John Boulderson, sailed

Green Bank quay viewed from the Flushing side, with two ferry boats. A detail from Jan Brandes, *The Kai af Falmouth, June 1778*. [Rijksmuseum, Amsterdam]

from Portsmouth as fourth mate on the East Indiaman *Marquis of Lansdown*, bound for Bengal.[82] The commander was the boy's uncle Joseph Boulderson, who had left the packet service and advanced himself by marrying the daughter of a prosperous London corn merchant. He was now making his way up the ranks of the East India Company. The Bouldersons' second son Leslie was in the Royal Navy; having entered as an able seaman on HMS *Bellerophon* at the age of 15, within a month he was made a midshipman. He was at the Battle of the Nile in 1798, and would retire as a commander.

John Philips Boulderson died on 24 November 1797, leaving his quarter share in the *Earl of Halifax* to his son John. As well as his country house at Boswarren he owned copyhold premises in Falmouth (probably a house in Mulberry Square), and was also part-owner of his son John's house at Bareppa in the parish of Mawnan, and of a barton or farm at Trewin. His death earned a few lines in *The Times*. 'On the 24th inst. at his house, at Boswarne, near Falmouth, John Boulderson, the elder, aged 82 years, a well respected and worthy member of Society, and many years Commander of one of his Majesty's Packets on the Falmouth station.'[83]

The ransom of the Prince Adolphus

On 9 June 1798, three days out from Lisbon, the *Prince Adolphus* was chased for some hours off Cape Finisterre by a prolific French privateer from Morlaix named *Le Tigre*, which captured the packet without a fight and took off most of the crew, including Captain Boulderson. The passengers were left on board the packet pending ransom negotiations. The story of what happened next led the maritime news in the *Caledonian Mercury*, ahead of the manoeuvres of Earl St Vincent and Admiral Nelson.

> Lisbon, June 24. 1798. The Prince Adolphus Packet, which sailed from this place for Falmouth about 15 days ago, was captured, 150 leagues to the westward of Cape Finisterre, by a French privateer of 18 guns (Le Tigre of Morlaix), after a few hours chace, no resistance being made by the packet. The subsequent circumstances of this capture are novel and curious. The passengers consisted of General Pigot and his Lady from Gibraltar, with upwards of twenty officers in the army, besides ten other passengers. The Captain of the privateer came on board the packet; he assured the passengers that they might make themselves perfectly easy, that there were two sorts of privateers sailed from France. Some were pirates, but he was not of that description. — The Captain of the packet, and the crew, except the steward, he put on board the privateer; but told the passengers that if they gave him their word of honour that they would not retake the packet, he would let them remain on board, and he left on board only a prizemaster, four men and six boys; he did not examine the passengers nor disarm the officers. The Captain of the packet wished to ransom her, but the citizen asked 800 l. which he would not comply with. The privateer continued her cruize, directing the prize to make the first port in Spain; after being three days at sea, the passengers agreed with the prize-master to ransom her for 17,000 dollars, and to return to this port, where she arrived yesterday.[84]

It was a curious episode. The writer omits to mention that the packet's surgeon, John Bullocke, was among the crew members who were left on board the *Prince Adolphus*. It was Bullocke who reported back to the Falmouth packet agent, Benjamin Pender, when they reached Lisbon on 16 June.

> I have to inform you of the Capture of his Majestys Packet Prince Adolphus which was taken on Saturday the ninth Inst: six days after we left Lisbon in Lat: 42°:58′ No. and Long. 15°:45′ We. of London, by Le Tigre a French Brig Privateer mounting 14 Nine Pounders, 2 Brass Twelves, and 95 Men; Commanded by Citizen Marie Peijrusset: — previous to our surrender the Mail and Dispatches were thrown overboard and sunk.[85]

The surgeon reported that Captain Boulderson with most of his officers and crew had been taken on board the privateer, together with one of the passengers who was master of the *Aurora* frigate; he appended a passenger list. Captain Peijrusset had put a prize master and 13 men on board the packet, with orders to proceed to the first French or Spanish port he could make. From Bullocke's account it is clear that the prize master himself was now in trouble.

> Five days after the Privateer left us, the Wind being strong at North East and very bad Weather, the Prize Master declaring under these Circumstances, he knew not where to go, or what to do with the Ship, The Passengers proposed to him to sell the Ship and deliver her up at Lisbon, which he agreed to do, if I would become bound for the payment of the sum of Seventeen Thousand Dollars – being ignorant of any Act of Parliament existing against such proceedings, but on the Contrary supposing it perfectly legal, and being well acquainted with the present scarcity of Packets, conceived it a very advantageous purchase both for their Lordships the Post Master General and Owners, I was induced to comply, and in consequence arrived here this morning when the Ship was immediately delivered up to me; but to my great surprize was informed that what I had done was contrary to the laws of England.[86]

The surgeon had fallen foul of a five-year-old act of parliament that no-one seemed to be aware of except the packet agent at Lisbon,

Thomas Gonne, who was a wine merchant (and serial complainer about the inadequacy of his Post Office pay rate). As it happened, the passengers from the *Prince Adolphus* now stranded at Lisbon massively outranked and presumably outgunned everyone else concerned. Major-General Henry Pigot, commander of the garrison at Gibraltar, was accompanied by three colonels, three majors and two junior officers. Also on board were Mrs Pigot, three female servants, a child, and merchants from Seville and Cadiz who were probably Irish. Altogether there were 29 of them.

The hapless French prize master was released by the British navy commissioner at Lisbon, Isaac Coffin, 'in the absence of Earl St Vincent'. Pigot presented this as the fulfilment of the debt of honour owed by the passengers to the prize master who had agreed to bring the packet into an enemy port; it was the surgeon who was liable for the ransom, having signed a bond on 13 June. Nonetheless the general, his officers and the two merchants co-signed a letter to the British envoy to Portugal, Robert Walpole, asking him to intervene to secure the payment. The conduct of the captain of *Le Tigre* and all his officers was 'honorable in the extreme', and it would be 'honorable to the National Character and faith, prevent the ill treatment of such of his Majestys subjects as may be hereafter captured under similar Circumstances (particularly Captn Boulderson and the Crew of the Prince Adolphus now in the possession of the Enemy) and will benefit the Commerce of the British Nation by the immediate use of the Packet'.[87]

Pigot added this clincher: 'From the Rank that many of the undersigned hold in the Army it is almost unnecessary to recall to your remembrance the disagreeable situation in which they would have been placed, and the number of Men which would probably have been required for their Ransom, had they remained Prisoners with the Enemy.' Walpole sympathised but was in bed with a fever and in any case had no power to advance money without a Treasury order. Gonne wrote to the Post Office secretary Francis Freeling for instructions on how to proceed.[88]

The passengers probably crossed over to England on the *Walsingham* packet along with the letters from Lisbon. These reached Freeling's office in London on 5 July, as did Pender's report from Falmouth enclosing Bullocke's letter and the ransom papers. Three days later a formal letter went to the Lords Commissioners of the Treasury over the signatures of the Postmaster General, enclosing the papers in the case. The view from the Post Office was that, notwithstanding the clear legal infraction, the ransom should be paid and if necessary an act passed in Parliament to protect Mr Bullocke from being sued. This was their argument:

> We are fully satisfied that the Surgeon of the Packet was entirely ignorant of the legal Objections to which his Agreement with the French Prize Master is liable, and that he acted from the purest & most laudable Motives. It further appears to Us that the essential Point of National Faith is engaged in maintaining the Agreement. If this had been a doubtful Question the humane and very liberal conduct of the Captor would have had great weight with Us. But We cannot feel any doubt upon the Subject, and We are anxious to relieve the Minds of the respectable Officers & Passengers who are now liberated by virtue of the Agreement and who from a due sense of honor would be placed under a most severe embarrassment, if the stipulations to which they owe their Release were not strictly performed.[89]

Then there was the question of the merchandise on board. The agent Gonne had sent his own report of events to Freeling (with the ransom price inflated by the commission he himself would take). The prize master had orders from the privateer captain to proceed to Vigo,

> but owing to very strong Northerly Winds they could not gain that Port altho' several attempts were made, it appears the Passengers availing of this circumstance, prevailed on the Prize Master to ransom the Packet for the Sum of eighteen thousand hard dollars, to be paid within Six days after her safe arrival in the Tagus, for which Sum a Bond or Bonds were Signed by Mr. John Bullock the Surgeon in behalf of Captn. Boulderson, she arrived here the 16th Instant when the said Mr. Bullock applied to a

particular friend of Capn. Boulderson to advance that Sum, which was refused, he then applied to me alledging, that in consequence of the Capture, Government must reimburse Captn. Boulderson the estimated value of the Packet [...] but as he could not give me any Security I have declined interfering for the present, and more particularly so as I consider the whole proceeding to be illegal.[90]

Gonne added: 'Commissioner Coffin has taken her under his protection and put an experienced and confidential person on board to prevent any embezzlement of the Stores, and that no illicit trade may be carried on, it is reported she has Goods on board to the amount of £4000 Stg.' The identity of Captain Boulderson's particular friend is not known; nor is it clear who owned the merchandise, although one might guess that some of it was on consignment with the merchants on board. The Postmaster General had proposed to the Treasury that, after approving payment of the ransom to the prize master, they should 'settle with the Parties who had Merchandize on board and with the Underwriters the respective Proportions to be paid by them in diminution of our disbursements'.[91]

General Sir Henry Pigot, dashingly
portrayed by Francis Wheatley
in 1782

On 4 August the Treasury approved the payment. The ransom of 17,000 *piastres fortes* (Spanish dollars or pieces-of-eight) amounted to about £4,250, the maximum that the Post Office would itself have paid out in compensation for the loss of the packet, but the cost to the Treasury was much less, being offset by the auction in Lisbon of the goods on board. As Freeling (above the signatures of the Postmaster General) noted afterwards,

> a saving has been made in the Revenue to the amount of £2331. 13. 8. as We should have been liable to reimburse the Owners of the Packet to the full amount of her valuation (being £4,000) had she been taken into an Enemy's Port. By confirming the terms of the Ransom the National Faith has been preserved, and the Captors have expressed the greatest satisfaction at the honorable treatment which they have experienced, and have promised to interest themselves to obtain a speedy liberation of the Captain of the Prince Adolphus.[92]

By 5 September Gonne had paid the ransom, and the master of the *Prince Adolphus*, Henry Fenner, was in Lisbon and ready to sail with the packet for Falmouth. Gonne told Freeling that the French agent Monsieur Lafargue assured him he had written to the Minister of the Marine and to the French consul at Corunna and Vigo regarding Captain Boulderson, and both Lafargue and the prize master had given their word of honour he would be liberated immediately on his arrival either in France or in Spain.[93]

It did not happen. *Le Tigre* was in turn captured by HMS *Naiad* on 11 August, but the prisoners taken from the *Prince Adolphus* had evidently been put on shore before then. Captain Boulderson's name appears in January on a French prisoner exchange list at Mézières on eight weeks' honour, although the list gives no capture date. He was one of a group of officers sent on the *Union* cartel from Gravelines for Dover on 13 January 1799.[94]

Boulderson's decision not to resist capture after failing to outsail the attacker had paid off. He had preserved his new vessel intact, no-one was killed, and little time was lost by the packet service. That so many passengers were on board with their possessions may also have influenced his decision, making it near-impossible to clear the deck for a fight. The number of passengers seems extraordinary, given the standard packet design introduced in the early 1790s, which had just six small passenger cubicles. If the French captain – 'the citizen' – had taken them on board his vessel he would have had to accommodate them all. It also illustrates how profitable the Lisbon service was for packet commanders, for whom passenger fares were a direct source of income.

John Boulderson's family, and in particular the younger siblings at home in Falmouth, would have endured a wait with no news of their father, and then difficult news. The *Prince Adolphus* sailed for Lisbon on 20 May. Word reached Falmouth on 24 June (brought by the *Spy* sloop of war from Plymouth) that the packet was taken and that Captain Boulderson was on board the privateer. By then its capture must have been suspected; the next Lisbon packet, the *Prince of Wales*, had already arrived home on 22 June, after leaving Lisbon the day before the *Prince Adolphus* reappeared there.

At the time, John and Mary Boulderson's eldest son John had been away at sea for over a year. The *Marquis of Lansdown* arrived back in the Thames from Bengal in July 1798 by way of St Helena and the Cove of Cork, a month after his father was captured. Their second son Leslie was in the Mediterranean as a midshipman on HMS *Bellerophon*, Egypt ahead of him. On the day the *Prince Adolphus* was captured, Nelson and his fleet were off Malta, searching for Bonaparte. Two months after his victory in the Battle of the Nile, Nelson's dispatches reached London and were printed in the *London Gazette Extraordinary* of 2 October, with a list of officers killed and wounded – happily midshipman Boulderson was not among them. The families of mariners could be nothing other than stoical about the hazards of life, and Falmouth was a town populated by mariners. Mary Boulderson herself had crossed the Atlantic in wartime, and the children were perhaps raised to meet fears with fortitude. But still.

By September the *Prince Adolphus* was back on the Falmouth to Lisbon route under Henry Fenner, and when the packet left Falmouth with the Lisbon mails on 6 January 1799 under Captain Boulderson, it would have been the son, going as master. The *Prince Adolphus* remained on the Lisbon station for another 18 months, but John Boulderson II was ready to retire from the sea 'on account of declining health from long Services and Captivity when taken Prisoner in the Halifax'.[95]

He may also have wished to concern himself with the upbringing of his younger children, perhaps remembering the years he and his siblings had remained in London with their mother while their own father first worked on the Falmouth packets. The packet commander Edward Lawrance described his mixed feelings in 1776 on being put back into Falmouth for want of a favourable wind. It was vexatious, but 'when I reflect that a separation of five or six long months was so near at hand, which wd. part me from all I loved, what pleasure I say must one feel in once more spending an Evening with her I hold most dear and once more hear the prattling of my dear little ones'.[96]

John Boulderson II formally retired in April 1800 at the age of 50, to lead the life of a gentleman of substance at his house in the country at Bareppa, four miles south of Falmouth. His eldest son John, now almost 21, was appointed by the Post Office to replace him, as the third John Boulderson to command a Falmouth packet. Although he may already have sailed the *Prince Adolphus* on the Lisbon route for his father, as a junior captain he was ineligible to be appointed to that service and a month later Captain Robert Lea Jones took a half share in the *Prince Adolphus* and succeeded the elder Boulderson on the Lisbon station.

Captain John Boulderson the third

The third John Boulderson (1779–1838) first entered the packet service as a boy of around 12 on his father's vessel, the *Earl of Halifax*; he sailed on two transatlantic voyages, to New York and possibly to the West India islands.[97] In 1793, early in the French Revolutionary wars, his uncle Joseph Boulderson took him on as a midshipman on the East Indiaman *Marquis of Lansdown*. The boy now saw a wider world than his father or grandfather had ever navigated. The ship cleared Gravesend in May and sailed from Portsmouth with the fleet just before he turned 14. They reached Madras (Chennai) in September that year, and Diamond Harbour for Calcutta (Kolkata) in November. They remained in the Hooghly river until March 1794 when they sailed again for England, calling at St Helena in June and coming to moorings at Blackwall in September.[98]

Midshipman Boulderson may also have seen the impress crew that tried to board at Gravesend at the start of the voyage, but was repelled by the *Marquis of Lansdown*'s men and by soldiers on board bound for India (who broke open the arms chest for that purpose). He would have been on board when the India merchant fleet under convoy of Admiral Hood's Mediterranean fleet passed secretly down the English Channel at night, with no lights showing. He saw squalls and stormy weather in the southern ocean, a seaman flogged at St Helena for drunkenness and insolence; he saw a press lieutenant take off 14 men at Dover when they were almost home. John Boulderson sailed twice more to India on the *Marquis of Lansdown* under his uncle's command, as 6th and then 4th mate, and during the winter of 1796–97, in between those two voyages, he went as mate on the *Prince of Wales*, a Lisbon packet commanded by Lovell Todd.[99]

On 27 May 1800 John Boulderson III was commissioned to sail between Falmouth, the West Indies and North America in command of a newly-built vessel, the *Duke of Cumberland*. In fact the packet was still on the stocks at the Symons brothers' yard, only half built.

In March 1800 she was 'in her frames' according to John Burnett Bennott, the Post Office packet inspector; he noted on 6 November that year that she was 'lately launched'.[100] But on 25 November the secretary of the Post Office, Francis Freeling, wrote a severe letter to their agent Benjamin Pender in Falmouth:

> With respect to the Conduct of Captain Boulderson you will inform that Gentleman that the most decided Exertions are expected from him in expediting his Ship for the American Mail, and acquaint him that I cannot shew him a greater Indulgence than by forbearing to lay his letter before My Lords The Postmaster General, who would most assuredly comment severely on the extreme Delay of fitting out his Packet for which more than ample Time has been allowed since the Vessel was launched.[101]

The packet was expected to sail on 3 December with the New York mail. But that day Pender's deputy, William Gay, reported to Freeling:

> the Duke of Cumberland Packet is not yet afloat Capt Boulderson was in great hopes of getting her off this morning which was the highest Tide for the spring, but it did not flow enough by Eighteen Inches, therefore she cannot be got off till next spring tide, which will be about the 14 Instant and it will take a week or 10 Days to compleat her for Sea after she is afloat her Yards and Topmasts were taken on shore yesterday in order to lighten her, but without effect.[102]

Freeling suspected that the delay originated in Captain Boulderson's 'fear that the ship would have to proceed to America'. To Pender he wrote: 'I received your letter of the 3d Instant and am much surprised at the Conduct of Captain Boulderson in suffering his Ship to be beneaped, particularly after the Caution given him by Mr Bennet on the Subject when at Falmouth.'[103]

The delayed December mail was to be carried by the *Harlequin*, a temporary packet hired by Robert Lea Jones, who had begun the building of the *Duke of Cumberland* and retained a half share in her; the elder Boulderson took the other half.

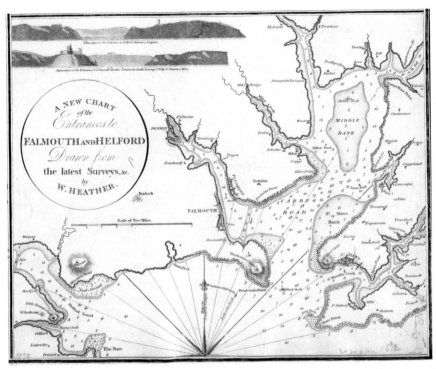

William Heather, *Chart of the entrances to Falmouth and Helford*, 1798 [Boston Public Library]

The *Duke of Cumberland* was registered in Falmouth on 17 January 1801, and six days later John Boulderson III sailed from there on his first transatlantic command, reaching New York in 35 days; on the return run via Halifax he crossed the Atlantic in 25 days. Less than fifteen months later the Treaty of Amiens brought a temporary halt to hostilities between Britain and France. After two West Indies voyages and one more to New York and Halifax, Captain Boulderson and the *Duke of Cumberland* were deemed surplus to peacetime requirements and retired from the service.

The Post Office did however express a sense of obligation 'to purchase of one of the Captains reduced by the Peace the Duke of Cumberland Packet Boat, which the Commander had built, and

65

introduced into the Service, on the faith of this Office'.[104] The younger Boulderson now mounted a public campaign on his own behalf. On 21 August 1802 an expression of support appeared in the *Cornwall Gazette* from seven passengers just arrived at Falmouth from New York and Halifax on the *Duke of Cumberland*:

> Mrs. Jennings and Son, Miss Clarke, Mrs. Oben, Mr. Hannay, Rev. Mr. Coker, and Mr. Low – who desire us to make public their acknowledgements to Captain Boulderson, for his polite attentions during the passage, and their regret that the arrangements made at the Post-office in consequence of the peace, should exclude him, as a junior Captain, from the service; which they cannot but consider as a public loss.[105]

This was followed a week later by an endorsement from his crew:

> We, the Ship's Company of his Majesty's Packet Duke of Cumberland, commanded by Capt. Boulderson, take this public method of expressing our unanimous Thanks to the said Capt. Boulderson, for the manly and proper treatment we have always experienced from him. We regret his leaving the service; and shall be happy at any future period to sail under his command. Signed, on behalf of the Ship's Company, Thomas Rapson, William Pearce.[106]

On the day that notice was published, a week after he arrived from Halifax, Boulderson left Falmouth again with the *Duke of Cumberland* bound for London (presumably also bearing two issues of the *Cornwall Gazette*). By 15 September his vessel was lying in Greenland Dock at Rotherhithe, to be bought in by the Post Office for £3,600.[107] He was ashore for barely a year. In 1803 the Peace of Amiens broke down, Britain declared war on the French Republic, and on 24 August Captain Boulderson was recommissioned on the West Indies and North America station, now back on his father's old ship the *Prince Adolphus* following the death of Robert Lea Jones, while the *Duke of Cumberland* was sold by the Post Office to Edward Lawrance and also returned to that service.

Joshua Johnson, *Portrait of a Gentleman,* *c.* 1805–15 [American Museum in Britain]. Thought to be Daniel Coker of Baltimore, who was born to a white indentured servant and an enslaved African American, became a Methodist Episcopal deacon, actively opposed slavery and was later a missionary in Sierra Leone. He was probably the Rev. Mr Coker who was a passenger on the *Duke of Cumberland.*

The *Prince Adolphus* endured no enemy engagements during this latest war, but the West Indies route was subject to a different hazard: yellow fever and malaria were endemic in the islands. When the packet arrived back in Falmouth in October 1804, four of the crew had been lost to the fever during the passage. The ship was quarantined, and before the mail was sent on to London it was fumigated, in a procedure of doubtful utility as Tony Pawlyn has noted: 'the folded letters were cut through in several places, fumigated, and soaked in vinegar. Just how effective this practice was is very uncertain. It certainly rendered the addresses and contents of many letters almost indecipherable.'[108]

On 8 May 1805, while another captain sailed with the *Prince Adolphus*, John Boulderson III got married. Mary Anne Carne was the daughter of a substantial Falmouth merchant by the name of John Carne who, like his father Richard before him, was also the East India Company's agent there.[109] It would no doubt have been through the Carnes that John Boulderson's upwardly mobile uncle Joseph Boulderson transferred from the packet service to the East India fleet.

Joseph Boulderson and the East India Company

In 1786 when John Carne was East India Company agent, Joseph Boulderson (1764–1828) was taken on as second mate on a Company vessel named the *Pigot*, aged 23. He had been going sea for 10 years, 'in several of his Majesty's Packets to America, the West Indies & Lisbon', as apprentice, as mate, then as master and temporary captain. Much of that is attested to, bitterly, by Samuel Kelly. It would have been Joseph's eldest brother John who first took him to sea as a boy on the packets.[110]

After a season as first mate on the *Pigot*, Joseph got his first East India command, for the third voyage of the *Marquis of Lansdown* in 1793–94, and brought along his nephew John as a midshipman. The previous year Joseph had married Sarah, daughter of a London corn factor named William Morley; the latter now retired to his country estate at Green Street House in East Ham, where a tower provided a view of the Thames. The house lay just three miles from the East India Company's shipyard at Blackwall, but Morley himself was in the coastal trade, with property at Barton upon Humber and granary in Rotherhithe at Cuckold's Point.

By 1807 William Morley's wife Sarah was evidently dead, since that year, at the age of 68, he married 26-year-old Sarah Crook, 'an amiable young woman of colour'.[111] In a codicil to his 1830 will added just before his own death in 1832, he reduced the bequests to his Boulderson grandchildren in favour of the children of his son William, Sarah's twin, adding this opaque explanation: 'as to Sarah Boulderson my daughter she is already amply provided for. This codicil it is my Wish that my Executors will particularly attend to it – the reasons are to myself'. We can only guess.

Joseph – although not his father-in-law – was an investor in an early Thames tunnel proposal between Gravesend and Tilbury. The man who launched the scheme in 1798 was the versatile Ralph Dodd, an artist turned engineer, and its failure four years later due to flooding and other disasters resulted in a loss to shareholders of £15,000. It could have been his wife's marriage settlement that provided Joseph with the funds to speculate.

Joseph's final voyage to the East Indies was during 1801–02 as commander of the *Fort William*. In 1804 he was appointed superintendent of the newly-built London Dock, which opened the following year at Wapping and was a private enterprise by a group of merchants, shippers and bankers. A contemporary engraving of the grand opening features a top-hatted figure standing on the deck of a merchantman about to enter the dock, who is evidently the superintendent – there is a marked resemblance to Joseph's portrait by Arthur William Devis. The magnifico beside him wearing a garter star must be Earl Camden, secretary of state for war and the colonies and principal guest at the festivities, who here appears to be pointing to a flag-bedecked ship inside the dock (a second view of the same vessel, since only a single ship featured in the ceremony, the *London Packet* from Oporto, flying flags of many nations).[112]

A closer look at the print raises a suspicion of artistic sniggering. The superintendent seems to have his hand cupped for a backhander from the earl, who may in fact be pointing to the young women prettily arranged on the dock wall, rather than to the ship in – and yet not in – the dock. The artist was Edward Francis Burney, who worked mainly as an illustrator but also produced some notable satirical watercolours. However, if this print is indeed a nod to contemporary gossip, it is lost to us now.[113]

Of the seafaring Bouldersons, Joseph alone is known to have had his portrait done. He most probably already knew Devis, who had been employed as a draughtsman on board an East Indiaman to make maps of South China Sea islands. After surviving a shipwreck, Devis went on to conduct a portrait practice in Calcutta before returning to England in 1795. Joseph's portrait shows him as a merchant captain, with a map and some folded letters at his side.[114] It could have been commissioned to mark his retirement from seagoing at the age

A view of the opening of the London Docks Wapping on the 31st January 1805, after Edward Francis Burney, 1805

of 40, although he looks older and it was probably done later. To be depicted by a man who had painted Nelson and George III may have appealed to him. He remained at Wapping dock for four years, waiting his turn for a senior shorebound vacancy at East India House. It came in August 1808 when he was appointed master attendant of shipping.

It may have been in that capacity, if not earlier, that Joseph first encountered a Humberside timber merchant, shipbuilder and ship-owner named John Barkworth.[115] Eight years later Joseph's daughter Emma married Barkworth's son John, who had recently inherited a substantial fortune from his father. It was on Humberside that Joseph Boulderson unexpectedly met his end. On 8 September 1828 he went out from his daughter's house in Hessle to go partridge shooting at Barton upon Humber south of the river, and there 'in the act of putting his gun to his shoulder, he fell down and expired instantaneously', according to a report in the *London Star*. He was still in office, and his wife Sarah was still living, although not necessarily with her husband. Joseph's will, like her father's four years later, cut her off with nothing.[116] Joseph instructed that he wished to be buried in his private family vault at East Ham, unless the cost of transporting his body there would exceed £100. Clearly that was so since they buried him at Hessle.

At his death Joseph Boulderson's address was John Street in Bloomsbury; he had acquired a property at Wotton in Surrey at about the time he became master attendant, but seems never to have lived there.[117] His widow, the former Sarah Morley, died in Exeter in 1845. When Joseph retired from the sea, about two years after the birth of their youngest child in East Ham, the couple may already have parted; he had a London address by 1799. If there was some scandal or unpleasantness (I have found no evidence), it does not appear to have come to William Morley's notice until much later, just before his death.

It is not at all clear what Sarah was doing in the decades before her death; she may well have been involved with her grandchildren in the west of England. In 1841 eight-year-old Shadwell Money Boulderson was living near Bideford in Devon. He was born in India to her son Shadwell Morley Boulderson, an East India Company employee, and his wife Louisa Anne Money.[118] Now the boy was in the household of a young man named William Gordon, together with an unrelated child and two female servants, one of whom Gordon married that

Arthur William Devis (1762–1822),
Portrait of Captain Joseph Boulderson,
c. 1808–1822. [Ferens Art Gallery, Hull]

year; this couple named their firstborn Cosmo Percy Boulderson Gordon (it appears that William Gordon later remarried bigamously).

Shadwell and Louisa Boulderson had already returned from India by 1840. They settled near Inverness in Scotland, first in Brahan Castle where further children were born, then in Erchless Castle. Young Shadwell Money was probably sent home from India in early childhood, either to be educated or because he was sickly, but he did not join his parents in Scotland. In 1847 at the age of 14 he died of tuberculosis in Brislington lunatic asylum near Bristol. Curiously, a portrait of him survives; he has a gentle, likeable face, looks maybe a little older, and wears a tartan waistcoat under a dark coat with a slash of red on the chest. It was probably painted posthumously.[119]

Another grandchild, Mary Gordon Boulderson, nine-year-old daughter of Shadwell's brother Henry, died of hydrocephalus at an Exeter boarding school in 1849. She too was probably born in India, where her father was also in the Bengal civil service. This family, so long entrenched within the East India Company, seems indelibly marked by the estrangements generated within the British colonial system. A nation that enforced vast imperial power overseas managed in the process to damage itself, in ways that the intermittent separations that were part of Atlantic mariners' lives did not.

Shadwell Money Boulderson

War fever in America

With Joseph dispatched we can go back to his nephew's career. After skipping a voyage to get married, John Boulderson III's next crossing was in October 1805 to New York. Then, after a couple of unremarkable years sailing the *Prince Adolphus* on the North America and West India routes, in 1807 he managed to provoke a miniature international incident off the New Jersey coast.

That year, as part of a mutual campaign of economic warfare, Britain was blockading France. British warships were deployed in Chesapeake Bay to prevent French vessels from maintaining trade with the United States, and Britain also asserted a right to search neutral vessels for deserters. On 7 March four seamen had deserted British navy ships in Hampton Roads off Norfolk, Virginia, and enlisted on the US navy frigate *Chesapeake*. The British warship *Leopard* was sent by the commander at Halifax, Admiral Berkeley, to get them back. On 22 June when the *Chesapeake* next put to sea, once the frigate was clear of the bay the *Leopard* hailed it. The commander of the *Chesapeake* refused to permit a search, upon which *Leopard* opened fire on the unprepared American vessel and fired three broadsides. The *Chesapeake* now surrendered, with three dead, 18 wounded and much damage, and the British commander sent a boarding party to retrieve the deserters by force.[120]

It turned out that three of the four men they caught and brought to Halifax were American-born citizens who had been pressed into the British navy. The men were court-martialled there on 26 August, and the sole British subject was hanged; a sentence on the others of 500 lashes was later commuted, reparations were paid and they were returned to the United States. But American public opinion was outraged by the insult to United States sovereignty. The inhabitants of Hampton destroyed 200 water casks destined for British men of war, a public meeting was called in New York, and President Jefferson prohibited British warships from entering United States ports.

Into this seething ferment sailed Captain Boulderson with the *Prince Adolphus*. On 19 August 1807 the packet was south of Sandy Hook on the approach to New York harbour, coming from Halifax. According to an indignant letter from a Mr Washington Morton to the editor of the *American Citizen*, the packet came alongside Morton's yacht and fired a gun without shot, then after 10 or 12 minutes another, with shot, which he estimated fell 50 or 100 yards to his stern; the boys on the end of the boom handing out the main-sail said it was a stone's throw. Morton understood the packet had called at Halifax and would therefore know the situation between the two nations, thus 'it might have been expected that some delicacy would have been observed to our national sovereignty and to our pilots'.[121] Captain Boulderson's reply followed in the *Citizen* the next day:

> His Majesty's Packet Prince Adolphus, New York, 21st Aug. 1807.
> Sir, In consequence of a publication in your paper of this day signed Washington Morton, I feel it a duty I owe the public and myself to make the following statement of facts as they occurred. On Wednesday afternoon, steering for Sandy Hook within five or six miles of the Light House, saw a schooner, built and rigged exactly in the pilot boat style: the wind being light with a flood tide, my anxiety was of course great to have a pilot on board. A signal was hoisted and a gun fired, which not being noticed fired another gun some minutes after; being shotted I directed the master to be very careful to point the gun very wide of her, in a direction that would be impossible to do any mischief, as evidently appears from the ball falling four or five hundred yards astern of the said schooner.[122]

He appended a sworn supporting statement from a US citizen who had come passenger with him from Halifax, who added that 'upon captain Boulderson's giving the master orders to fire the gun alluded to he replied, the shot will fall above a mile from her; the captain answered, better that than within twenty yards'.[123]

The packet had left Falmouth for Halifax and New York on 15 June, and on 4 July Captain Boulderson spoke to another vessel in

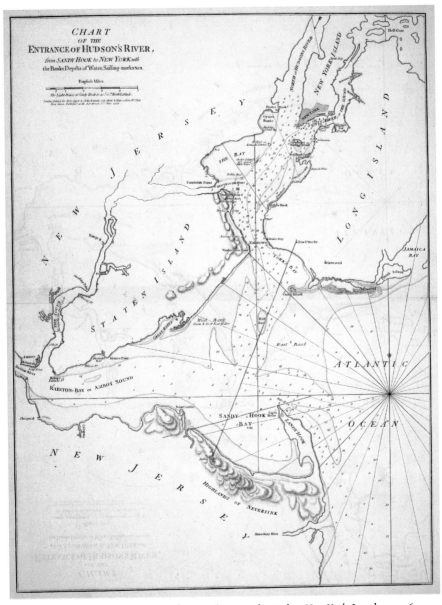

Chart of the entrance of Hudson's River, from Sandy Hook to New York, London 1776.
[New York Public Library]

Portraits of Cornelia Schuyler Morton and Washington Morton by Thomas Sully, 1807.
[Schuyler Mansion, Albany, New York]

longitude 46 west; on the same day, a British navy sloop came in to Halifax after a six-day passage from the Chesapeake with the news of the incident off the Capes of Virginia. The *Prince Adolphus* is said to have reached Halifax on 26 July (the day of the court-martial), and sailed from there for New York on 9 August. The time Boulderson spent waiting in the heart of the British North America squadron may have primed him for a combative and bad-tempered encounter, although his explanation seems believable enough.[124]

Washington Morton was an excitable New York attorney and, since he was the owner of a pleasure yacht, evidently a prosperous one – or at least one who had married well. He was also a Federalist and a brother-in-law to Alexander Hamilton. Correspondence and some editorial on the subject continued for a few days in the *New York Evening Post* and elsewhere. His wife Cornelia's brother Philip J Schuyler, who had been on board Morton's boat, stated (in prose less purple than Morton's) that after the shot was fired they went alongside the packet and the captain enquired if they intended to put a pilot on board, 'to which Mr Morton replied we were not a pilot-boat — The captain then said I know you now, and enquired how Mr M. did, to which Mr M. replied he was very well but that he did not thank him for the shot he had fired; and added, that if he had a twelve pounder on board he would get under his stern and make a sieve of him'.[125]

A New York pilot did eventually appear to bring the *Prince Adolphus* up to moorings, and to be cursed for his pains by Captain Boulderson as he went on board: 'You damn'd rascal you are come at last; you are like the rest of them, for they are all damn'd rascals.' This was reported by the *American Citizen*'s editor, who interviewed the pilot. This unfortunate man also got it in the neck from the editor, for assisting a British vessel.[126]

Interest in the affair soon fizzled out. While there were calls for British packets to be banned from New York harbour as potential spies, and Berkeley was recalled as a result of the *Chesapeake–Leopard* affair, Boulderson's return passage seems to have been uneventful. On 13 October he came in to Falmouth in 19 days from Halifax, bring-ing extensive newspaper accounts of the trial of the deserters taken out of the *Chesapeake*, and news of a failed mutiny in early September by most of the crew of the British frigate *Jason* off New York, who were said also to have been intent on desertion; their trial was in progress as he left Halifax. The episode off Sandy Hook must have rattled him nonetheless. The next voyage of the *Prince Adolphus* was to New York again, but he stayed at home. The events of that year, in one way or another, foreshadowed his downfall some years later.

The Falmouth packet seamen's strike

The *Prince Adolphus* continued on the transatlantic routes, usually with a substitute captain. In August 1809 the packet made the long passage to Brazil for the first time, with a navy escort through the Leeward Islands, arriving home the following February. On 1 July 1810 it was Captain Boulderson himself who set sail from Falmouth for the West Indies. In mid August while the *Prince Adolphus* was across the Atlantic, a crowd of packet crewmen in Falmouth gathered outside the office of the recently appointed Post Office packet agent there, Christopher Saverland, to request an increase in wages. Saverland described what happened to Freeling.

> This morning great numbers of the Sea Men, from all the Packets now in Port, assembled around my Office, when I requested Mr Williams, the Searcher, to tell them, if they would send one, or two Men, from each Ship, I should have no Objection to hear what they had to say, provided they conducted themselves in an orderly way. I saw them seperately from each Ship, when they represented, in a very proper submissive manner, the inadequacy of their Wages, to support their Families, requesting I would intercede in their behalf with the Postmaster General; and this afternoon the enclosed Petition was sent to me.[127]

The petition to the postmaster general stated: 'That your petitioners are not able to Support themselves and familys on the present Wages and allowance Money. Every thing being so exceeding Dear in this place as well the Necessarys of life as House Rent'. They asked for three pounds per month for a seaman, four pounds per month for a petty officer.[128]

Forwarding their petition to Freeling in London, Saverland remarked that since the Lisbon packets had been ordered not to carry out goods upon freight, 'the Seamen of those Packets have shewn much uneasiness'. He believed they had been working upon the minds of the other packet seamen, to obtain an increase of wages;

he also believed their pay was much lower than in other government services.[129] Freeling noted, in a minute to the postmaster general (Lords Chichester and Sandwich jointly), 'it will be a fortunate thing for the Post Office if the Lisbon packets may be licensed to carry merchandise – it will bring us £2000 a year Revenue, and *probably prevent a considerable encreased expenditure for Wages for Seamen*'.[130]

It was a well-established practice of the packetmen to supplement their inadequate government-mandated pay by illicit private trading, their 'little adventures', to which a blind eye was usually turned. In foreign ports they would acquire a wide assortment of goods and produce which they would carry home in their personal sea chests, bring ashore quietly and sell locally. They did likewise on outward runs, carrying goods on behalf of local merchants; the trade was woven into the local economy. Saverland wrote again adding his view that the request was reasonable, overseas markets were overstocked so seamen could not sell their wares there and their little adventures were seized by customs officers when brought home. He had seen this personally.[131] His letter crossed one from Freeling, who now set out the argument that the Post Office came to rely on:

> I almost doubt whether the Postmaster Genl, have any thing to do with the Seamen *individually*. The Contract is made by Their Lordships with *one* Person (the Commander) at an Establishment setting forth certain Allowances to Officers & Seamen and if there are any Difficulties on the Part of either as to Wages, it ought to be a Consideration *purely with the Contractor* and not *with the Office*.[132]

In Freeling's opinion they would hear no more of these applications since they must infallibly lead to reopening the contracts and putting them all up to auction. A threat, in other words, to the commanders. But his prediction was proved wrong.

The *Prince Adolphus* arrived home in Falmouth from the Leeward Islands on 30 September. On the morning of 24 October the packet was mustered with the mail and passengers on board, sails unfurled, and on the point of slipping moorings to sail for Cadiz and the Mediterranean, together with the *Duke of Marlborough* for Lisbon. The Falmouth customs officer picked that moment to crash into this tense and unresolved affair. Mr Platt and his men boarded the *Prince Adolphus*, broke open the seamen's private chests and seized their little adventures. Upon this the crew refused to put to sea. Saverland was brought on board but could not persuade them, even by threat of dismissal and loss of their protection against navy impressment.

The customs men repeated their operation on the *Duke of Marlborough*, whose crew also refused to sail. Saverland called in the navy in the person of Captain James Slade, the senior officer at Falmouth, and a navy lieutenant boarded the two packets with a press gang. With some difficulty, since Slade had only the crews of the impress boat and an excise cutter at hand, 26 seamen were eventually impressed and sent on board his own ship, HMS *Experiment*.[133]

An outraged Captain Slade reported these events to the Admiralty, adding: 'Two or three old Men behaved particularly ill, thinking their age would prevent their detention on board a Man of War: one of them drew his knife on me. I beg likewise to mention that Jno.

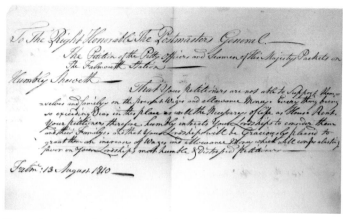

The packet seamen's petition to the Postmaster General, 13 August 1810
[Royal Mail Archive, POST 29/1]

Brewer (son to one of the Carpenters of the Packets) an apprentice to a Shipwright at Flushing was on board one of the Packets at the time, behaved particularly insolent to me, bidding me defiance, as his Indentures would protect him.'[134]

Slade termed it a mutiny, but realised he could not issue orders to the packet officers; like the men they were civilians employed by their commanders. He reported that he had taken out every man from the two packets, although in reality some of them probably got away in boats as the impress boat approached. Saverland had persuaded a few of the *Duke of Marlborough*'s men to remain at duty, and after Slade put 14 navy sailors on board the packet had crew enough to sail; but he could not spare any more for the *Prince Adolphus* so the Cadiz and Mediterranean mail was put on board a navy cutter. Saverland instructed Captain Boulderson to get his ship manned as soon as possible.

Next day the crews of the other packets in the harbour assembled in the court in front of Saverland's office to demand the release of their comrades from the *Experiment*. They sent in this note:

> Sir. We have assembled here to Request the Men which were Last Evening put Onboard the Experiment from the Duke of Marlbrough and the Prince Adolphis antill such time as the hire sent Onshore or Elite Onboard their Respective Ships we Cannot think of Doing any Duty Onboard our own Ships Sir In your getting Our Brothers releived to their Wives & Familys We Remain your Hble Servts[135]

The agent, bolstered by the opinions of Slade and of 'such of the Captains of the Packets as I have been able to consult', concluded that no concession should be made to the seamen until they returned to their duty. The packet inspector now also appeared on the scene, unhelpfully. 'Mr Bennett arrived last Night, & has been consulted respecting what has been done, but as our Opinions upon the subject do not accord, he has left me', wrote the fair-minded Saverland. This glimpse of the inspector's nature was echoed by Freeling in London:

'The Inspector of Packets is also at Falmouth, but I do not conceive that his presence there can in any degree allay the ferment'.[136]

Saverland, who agreed with the seamen's case for higher wages but not their actions, now found himself in a tight corner. The civil powers were summoned, the Riot Act was read and the crowd dispersed. The *Duke of Marlborough* with a mixed crew sailed later that day. Saverland wrote to Admiral Calder, the navy's commander-in-chief at Plymouth, expressing his hope that a reinforcement of seamen might be sent to Slade, and a vessel provided for the Surinam mail (HM schooner *Mullet* had put back for repairs). And for speed, he asked Calder if he would inform the government in London of the events in Falmouth using the latest Admiralty signalling system, the telegraph – not yet the electrical telegraph but the mechanical shutter relay, which had been extended to Plymouth in 1806 and took minutes to cover the distance rather than the usual two days by road.[137]

Next day, 26 October, the seamen did not risk appearing in the town but assembled on the bowling green on the hill above it, and now demanded both the release of the men on the *Experiment* and a wage increase. Saverland went on board the packets to muster them and found very few seamen other than the captains, masters, mates and a few boys. Clutching at straws, he thought perhaps if the government were to send down 200 pensioners from the Greenwich Hospital the mutiny would subside. Slade on the other hand expected a reinforcement of seamen from Plymouth, and Saverland was coming round to the navy officer's punitive view: 'should a Frigate fortunately put in, not a mutinous Packets Man will dare to show his rascally Head'.[138]

Another day on and Saverland had further disturbing news for Freeling. The previous evening the public cryer had gone round the streets of Flushing calling the packet men and lumpers (riggers) to a meeting that night at the Seven Stars, the object being to stop the lumpers from working on board the packets and to raise money to send two delegates to London. 'John Parker & — Pasco men of bad

Christopher Saverland, *c.* 1810, artist unknown (left), and Francis Freeling, *c.* 1830, by George Jones. [The Postal Museum]

Character set off this morning by the Mail Coach to state their Case to you. The Women who are always the most forward in these affairs have sent into the Country to persuade the Tinners to come to their Assistance'.[139] The tinners were local tin and copper miners, who had a history of uprisings over the high price of food, but there seems to be no evidence that they turned out for the seamen. Saverland enclosed a description of the delegates:

> Pasco (known at Falmouth by the name of Sir F. Burdett) formerly a steward of the Prince Wm. Henry under the command of Capt. Peters, afterwards an Officer of Excise but it is understood he was discharged for sedition or treasonous expressions. He now keeps a petty Grocers Shop in Falmouth [...] John Parker an America[n] by birth has been Steward on board several Packets lately does not stand high in point of character at present does not belong to any Ship is known to possess much low cunning and well inclined to promote mischief — Pasco is about 5 feet 6 inches high, about 50 Yrs of age near sighted — Parker is about 45 Yrs of age about 5 feet 6 inches high dark complexion'[140]

The packet captains and indeed the whole population of Falmouth were undoubtedly in sympathy with the packetmen's cause, since the town depended on the service. Anonymous threats were made against the customs men and also against Samuel Pellew, the local collector of customs.[141]

Slade wrote in a fury to the Admiralty secretary: 'yesterday I felicitated myself on having at last roused the Mayor and Magistrates to action, in prevailing on them to call in Military Aid and forcibly enter the Dwelling Houses of the Mutinous Packet Sailors for the purpose of impressing them or securing their Persons. I am sorry to say this has merely ended in the promise'. By four o'clock, the mutinous seamen were marching out through the country in large parties armed with large sticks. 'Not having received the smallest Assistance from the Captains of the Packets who bear a Commission in the Kings Service nor from their Officers', Slade had asked Saverland to send out the captains and officers with the impress lieutenant and constables to arrest the packet sailors. 'Instead of the Packet Captains being ordered the Masters were, and when they were called on by the Lieutenant on the Impress service to attend him, they refused going.' Saverland explained later that he had ordered the masters to go because they were the ones who knew where the seamen lived, but the masters had declined to go without their captains.[142]

By the time Richard Pascoe and John Parker arrived in London, Freeling knew they were coming and suggested to the Admiralty secretary, John Wilson Croker, that they should be impressed on arrival. When they showed up in Freeling's office, he refused to discuss their case and handed them over to a City marshal. They were locked up in the Poultry compter and next day appeared before the lord mayor at the Mansion House. From the record of that examination comes Pascoe's version of the events in Falmouth and his virtuous mission to present the seamen's case to government in person:

I am a Grocer — Last Wednesday Evening I heard there had been Disturbances on board the Marlborough, & that the Men had been put on board a Man of War, I said serve them right — on the Jubilee heard huzzaing, I ran — a great Number of Men, Women, and Children — it began to rain & I went Home, & in the afternoon I heard that the men had refused to serve any longer. I went to the Excise to swear to my Book — My Daughter came running — said the Petty Officers were at my House — that they had a Petition written by Walter Gillimore, Schoolmaster. — I went home, & then went to the Men at the old Bowling Green & spoke to them, perhaps 200 or 300 of them, belonging perhaps to ten or a dozen Packets — The Petition stated they had been robbed by the Customs — I did not like the word *robbed* — they asked if I would draw another Petition — I said I would go a hundred Miles to do the Government Service, as well as to serve them, I had Business in Town to Doctors' Commons — God is my Judge I did all I could for the Service.[143]

Two days later the attorney general ruled that as Pascoe and Parker had committed no offence in London the lord mayor could not act against them. But by then it had already been decided to move the entire Falmouth packet establishment and lodge it within the navy station at Plymouth. On 31 October Freeling called at the Home Office and at the Admiralty to make arrangements for Calder to have the packets brought round to Plymouth, and wrote to Saverland instructing him to proceed there himself with their commanders.

On 31 October Saverland wrote three times to Freeling. First he reported that the mayor of Falmouth had called a meeting of inhabitants the day before, and 'in consequence of his assurances that the greater part of the Seamen would return to their Duty if I would issue an Advertisement promising their being received, and protected, on board their several ships; I caused the enclosed advertisement to be printed and distributed'. Saverland excepted six men from his amnesty, whom he described as ringleaders, one of them being John Parker.[144]

Saverland was by then confident that the packetmen would return and order would be restored. In a private letter to Freeling the same day he wrote that if Freeling should hear anything of the removal of packets to Plymouth the report was Saverland's own, 'to raise the Falmouthians from the stupour & apathy with which they have witnessed (& even taken part) the mutinous Conduct of the rascally Packets Men'. It had the effect he wished and was the cause of the meeting yesterday. He had not been four months in the town and had witnessed three mutinies; he was sick and tired of the town and its inhabitants. He feared the captains would not advance wages at their own expense. Still unknown to him was that removal to Plymouth was no longer merely a threat.[145]

On 1 November a note arrived in his office, over the names of 25 packet crewmen and one apprentice (assuming the writer was John Brewer the carpenter and the first-named person was his son who had 'behaved particularly insolent' to Slade), all now being held on board the *Experiment*:

Experiment Octr 31st 1810
Sir we do are [hear] that you have granted liberty for all the packets men to joine their Ships which we hope you will except of us allso as we are all willing to join the Ships again we have ben along time in the sarvise and most of us have very large famelys & we will sine our names to this letter and we do hope that your honour will except of us
John Brewer S Jago Richard Eastwood John Bonds John Callaway
John Strike John Striker Thomas Rowe John Fittock Hugy Stephens
Matthew Bant John Eller John Bishop Samuel Woodcock
William Vivian Peter Rundle Alexander Peters Tobias James
Thomas Ball Thomas Scott William Vingo Michael Pascoe
William Oke John Smith Hanable Orchard,
Sir I Beg Parden for Sending this from your Humble Sirvent
John Brewer[146]

Next day Saverland began a letter to Freeling about his arrangements for manning the packets, including the *Prince Adolphus* which was still in harbour and short of a full crew:

The Seamen have returned to their duty. I had a full Muster this morning in all the Ships except the Prince Adolphous Capt. Boulderson, the greater part of his Ships Company being confined on board His Majestys Ship Experiment, but I trust she will be fully manned & ready to sail with the Mediteranean Mail on Monday next, before which time the Nocton will not be ready; & Captain Naylor giving up very handsomely that Mail to Captain Boulderson I was happy in letting the Adolphous go that Voyage for which she was fully prepared, & would otherwise have been a great loss to him.[147]

Before he finished writing, an express letter arrived from Freeling with orders to move.[148] The *Prince Adolphus* sailed from Falmouth for Malta on 4 November, with an able seaman taken from each of the packets in harbour making up the seven men she was short of. Now the agent had to relocate his staff and office in a hurry.

Saverland sailed for Plymouth on 6 November on HMS *North Star*, accompanied by a frigate, two sloops of war and a flotilla of packets, listed with their captains by his deputy William Gay, who remained in Falmouth: *Princess Elizabeth*, Kidd; *Nocton*, Naylor; *Express*, Bullock; *Diana*, James; *Dispatch*, Kirkness; *Adventure*, Tilly. The other packets in dock repairing and fitting for sea would follow when ready.[149] They reached Plymouth next day, where Calder ordered the packets into Hamoaze but could provide no officers' accommodation, so Saverland and his four staff installed themselves at the Fountain inn.

On the day the packets left Falmouth, the newly liberated Pascoe and Parker issued writs in London against Freeling 'for a trespass'. In Falmouth, Slade stood by his assertion that the mayor and magistrates had refused to assist him, adding his opinion that 'from the Mayor down to the most insignificant Person, all are connected to the Packets People either by Interest or consanguinity'. And he had received no assistance from any of the packet officers, with the exception of 'the gallant Capt. Rogers' who had persuaded his crew to return and proceeded to the West Indies.[150]

But Slade was beginning to regret his haste, and wrote privately to Saverland: 'By the inclosed you will see in what manner I am brought forward as a Public accuser'. He did not expect this when he wrote in the bitterness of his heart to give a detail to the Admiralty board of the disgraceful proceedings, and asked Saverland to pass on his request that the postmaster general would proceed no further with his complaint against the packet officers. Removal to Plymouth would be a sufficient punishment.[151]

While Saverland thought the town should be made to eat humble pie for a while, he endured numerous difficulties at Plymouth. The stoves and fumigating machines were not brought with them, as the packets were calling first at Falmouth anyway, although Calder was asking government to do away with fumigation except in case of quarantine. Passengers were in different inns, the custom house was two miles off, the packets were in different places, they lay badly there and there was difficulty with the purchase of anchors in very deep waters. Not a man of war went to sea without pilotage. There was no time advantage over Falmouth, and Plymouth was more expensive. He hoped the packets would not remain there as a fixed station.[152]

The packetmen were equally anxious. They were now obliged to live on board their vessels while they lay at Plymouth, and their livelihoods were at risk. From Falmouth another petition was sent in, signed by 125 of them belonging to eight packets.

We the undersigned Seamen belonging to the Packet Service having been among those whose late direlection from their duty has been the Cause of the removal of the Packets from Falmouth Humbly beg leave to assure your Lordships that we are impressed with a strong sense of the Impropriety of our Conduct on that occasion and are full of Sorrow and Contrition that we should have occasioned thereby any Interruption to his Majestys Service. — But we trust that when your Lordships are pleased to consider the Circumstances which led to our refusal to do our duty — the breaking open of the Chests when on the point of sailing, and the taking therefrom the little Adventures, we are induced to carry with us to enable us to provide for ourselves and our families — We trust that when your Lordships reflect on the impulse which must have been given to our feelings, that your Lordships will be pleased to attribute the

Circumstances which followed to the irritation of the moment. For the whole of our conduct on that occasion we are now extreamly repentant, and Humbly implore that your Lordships will be pleased to overlook the same, and to Permit the Packets to sail from Falmouth (where our Wives and families reside) as heretofore.[153]

The petition is dated 23 November 1810 and signed or marked by men belonging to the *Nocton, Express, Princess Elizabeth, Townsend, Marlborough, Adventure, Prince Ernest* and *Queen Charlotte*.

As the *Prince Adolphus* headed for Gibraltar and Malta, Walter Callaway wrote an anguished letter to the local MP Davies Giddy: 'Necesaty Drives me to trubel you with theas few lins. My son John have lernt Navagation and Enterd on board the Dolphins packit for Jubalalter and Molta'. The boy had only been on the *Prince Adolphus* three days and never been to sea when the packetmen refused to sail, and now he was on board the *Experiment*. His father petitioned for the Admiralty to clear him or order him back in the packet service.[154] Two days later comes a letter from young John Callaway himself, on board HMS *L'Aigle* in Plymouth Sound:

Dear father and Mother Hnd Brothers I am Now on Bord of the Le Eigal Now At Plymouth Sound And waiting for A fair Wind to Sail to Malta there Are Six Men Clear by their frends and if you have A Mind to Clear Me you Are better to try in Season for My Clearance but I dear say that I Shall be Carid to Malta first with out you have Cleard Me Already We Are 23 of us Now on bord of the Packets Men Now on board of the Le Eigal of 36 guns but we Shall Not Stay here Long In this Ship but Shall be put on bord of Some Man of war Soon We are All In Good health at Presant I have Nothing to Say More but I hope for My Clearance Soon & If I arnt Clear before I am pot on board of Aney Other Ship I will write you Again.[155]

Meanwhile a delegation of Falmouth worthies led by the mayor had travelled to London with a petition to the prime minister, Spencer Perceval, among them Captain Boulderson's father-in-law John

Carne. They were aghast at the utter ruin of Falmouth that would inevitably follow the loss of the packets. They were unable to shift government opinion then, but circumstances did it for them.

Plymouth turned out to be highly unsuitable as a packet station on numerous counts, and despite heavy lobbying by various interested parties for Fowey as a packet station, by the end of January 1811 the government had decided the packets should go back to Falmouth. The news that they were coming home was greeted by fireworks and bonfires. The *Prince Adolphus* arrived home to Falmouth from the Mediterranean on 4 February, Saverland was there by the 7th, and the packets came in from Plymouth under convoy on 15 February.

As for the legal suit by Pascoe and Parker against Freeling for a trespass, by early December Parker the American was on board HM sloop *Tyrian* at Falmouth bound for the Mediterranean, and wanted to give it up. Pascoe held out, saying he was a Roman and never would. A Falmouth Quaker named Mr Tregelles was acting as mediator and tried to persuade Pascoe to withdraw, although according to Saverland 'he is such a Villain it is most difficult to deal with him'.[156] In January Pascoe withdrew his suit. By then Freeling and his clerks had amassed a substantial bundle of papers relating to the mutiny. It may be thanks to Pascoe and Parker that this multifarious collection of documents survives, having been put together at the time and then abruptly laid aside.

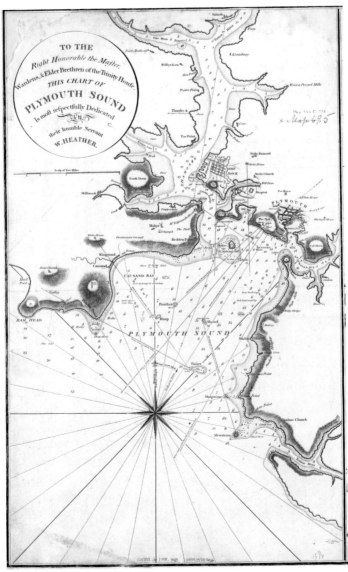

William Heather, *Chart of Plymouth Sound*, 1798 [Boston Public Library].
The Falmouth packets were initially assigned moorings near the navy
dock in Hamoaze and in Stonehouse Pool, then moved to Catwater,
the inlet at centre right of this chart.

The war of 1812

It was during the summer of 1812 that Captain Boulderson got himself into the newspapers again. On 28 May he sailed from Falmouth for Suriname in South America. On 5 July, within 50 miles of the Suriname river, the *Prince Adolphus* fell in with the *Pocahontas*, an American merchant schooner from Boston. The commander, Captain Randlett, said that while he was in the Cape Verde Isles to take on a cargo of salt, his vessel was hijacked by an American seaman escaped from impressment on a British man of war together with nine Portuguese convicts, all of whom were trying to get off the islands.

Randlett had later regained control of his vessel but was now out of provisions and feared his prisoners were planning to seize the schooner again. Both vessels anchored off the coast that night, and Captain Boulderson lent him firearms, cutlasses and ammunition. Next day *Pocahontas* kept company with *Prince Adolphus* upriver as far as Fort Amsterdam. Randlett was taken to be examined by the British authorities at Paramaribo, repaired his ship and was to proceed with his prisoners to Barbados under escort of a British navy sloop, the *Surinam*. As they waited at anchor in the mouth of the river for the tide to turn so they could sail, the British navy brig *Swaggerer* arrived with the news that their two countries were now at war.[157]

The *Prince Adolphus* was due to leave Suriname on 10 July, and is next seen about 250 miles up the coast at Georgetown, Demerara (now Guyana), where the governor, the paymaster and the collector of the colony embarked as passengers (Lord Liverpool had recalled governor Henry William Bentinck in April that year). The packet sailed from there on 19 July, heading for home by way of the Caribbean islands. It was billed to sail on 25 July from Barbados.[158]

The dates matter. After that there is a trace of the *Prince Adolphus* at Guadeloupe, reported later by Captain Rogers in the *Countess of Chichester* packet who was following the same route about two weeks behind, and sailed from Martinique on 13 August. But when the

Gerrit Schouten (1779–1839), *Diorama of the Waterfront of Paramaribo*, 1820 [Rijksmuseum, Amsterdam]. Europeans bought Schouten's dioramas as souvenirs, and he also produced botanical watercolours.

Chichester reached Falmouth on 13 September the *Prince Adolphus* was still not in. Rogers reported that a great many American privateers were cruising among the West India Islands, and had made a great many captures; the packet was feared taken.

In America its fate was already known. Six days before the *Chichester* arrived in Falmouth, the district court of Pennsylvania gave notice of the intended sale of 'Prince Adolphus, her tackle, apparel and furniture, and the goods, wares and merchandize laden therein'.[159] A week or so out from Martinique on about 9 August, the packet had been captured by the *Governor McKean* privateer schooner commanded by Captain Lucet, 'without a shot fired', and brought in to Philadelphia on 21 August.[160] A Philadelphia newspaper printed this presumably first-hand account of Captain Lucet's triumph:

Capt. Lucet of the Governor McKean privateer of this port, captured his Britannic majesty's Packet Prince Adolphus, & when his majesty's Captain observed the little paper sided schooner, he was mortified, and observed to Captain Lucet that if he had known the real force and quality of the Governor McKean, he would have sunk her — Captain Lucet coolly replied: 'My dear sir, I will make you very easy on that subject — secure to me $6000 as consideration for my prize, and I will restore her to you with all your men, *and then retake you.*' His majesty's Captain very politely and prudently declined hazarding his *poll* again.[161]

Details of Lucet's prize duly appeared in a Philadelphia auction notice:

On Thursday morning, the 1st of October next, at 10 o'clock, at Hozey's wharf, Queen street, the Cargo of the British Prize Ship Prince Adolphus, consisting of: Rum, Sugar, Coffee, Irish Beef and Pork, Noyeau in cases, Claret and Port Wine, Coal, Empty Bottles, Water Casks, Kentledge, Juak [junk], Shot different size, 4 six pound carronades, rammers, &c. Two 6 long guns complete, and sundry other articles. Also, on the same day, at 12 o'clock at noon, at the Merchants' Coffee House, in the city of Philadelphia, the said Ship Prince Adolphus, Together with her Tackle, Apparel and Furniture, as she now lies at Hozey's wharf.[162]

Not much of that inventory looks like merchandise – the rum, sugar, coffee and noyeau (almond liqueur) possibly; some of that could have been the property of the passengers. The presence on board of the party from Demerara provoked an excited press sub-head: 'A British Governor Taken! The privateer Governor Mc Kean, has captured and carried into the port of Philadelphia, the British packet, Prince Adolphus, of 18 guns and 36 men, bound from Martinique to Falmouth, E. having on board the Governor, Collector and Paymaster of Demerara'. Ship and tackle sold for $3,000.[163]

News of the capture of the *Prince Adolphus* was in London by 29 September, via an American cartel ship which had come in to Liverpool three days earlier. The *Nymph* packet arrived at Falmouth on 26 October with about half the crew of the *Prince Adolphus* on board, having left New York on 1 September and Halifax on the 9th; the captain had previously arrived. Captain Boulderson got home by way of Liverpool on the *Tontine* cartel, which sailed from Philadelphia on 20 August and reached Liverpool on 17 October, via New York.[164]

The report in the *Cornwall Gazette* of the return of the *Prince Adolphus*'s crew appeared immediately below the news that the *Princess Amelia* packet of six guns had been captured in the Caribbean on 15 September. It happened after a fierce fight in which Captain Moorsom, the master Mr Nankivell and a boy had all been killed, and ten crew members had been wounded including the mate. The paper also printed the mate's account of the action, written from the Downs to Saverland in Falmouth. The *Princess Amelia* had encountered a schooner some distance away and made the private signal with a gun, at which the stranger hoisted Spanish colours, tacked and headed towards them. Supposing her to be an enemy, when the schooner came in gunshot range Moorsom ordered a shot fired, upon which the schooner hoisted American colours and fired a broadside. After nearly an hour of heavy fighting and with both the master and then the captain dead, the packet was too crippled to continue, so sank the mail and struck her colours.[165]

The *Princess Amelia*'s attacker was a Baltimore privateer of 11 carriage guns and 95 crew. The business with the Spanish flag would have been to get in closer before the packet knew it was under attack; an outward-bound British ship might still be unaware that the two countries were now at war. In fact the *Princess Amelia* had called at Barbados on 16 August so Captain Moorsom already knew. More to the point, of course, was the fact that he defended the mails to the last, and Captain Boulderson in similar circumstances did not.

Boulderson knew about the war by the time he encountered the *Governor McKean*. He may well have left the Suriname river before the *Swaggerer* arrived there with the news, but on 25 July he was at Barbados and due to sail, four days after the *Barbados Mercury* received news of Madison's declaration of war and two days after it was confirmed. It had in any case come as little surprise. The *Barbados Mercury* also noted an unconfirmed rumour that two American privateers were cruising 'in these waters'.[166] Following the declaration of war, United States privateers had very swiftly fitted out to go hunting among the British merchantmen in the Caribbean; HM brig *Swaggerer* was one of the British vessels chasing them.

One of the captured passengers from the *Prince Adolphus* gave the story to the local newspaper in Demerara on his eventual return there in December.

> H. Frost, Esqr. [...] was a passenger hence, in the *Prince Adolphus* packet, already announced as captured; but to the particulars of which, we have hitherto been strangers. It now appears, however, that the Packet was taken by the American privateer *Governor McKean*, Lucat, commander, mounting six six-pounders and one long twelve, on the 8th of August; and that she was carried into Philadelphia on the 24th. But, the most extraordinary circumstance attending her loss — was the surrender of Capt. Boulderson, without firing a gun! — and that too, in defiance of the entreaties and remonstrances of the passengers and crew! — A conduct so disgraceful and uncommon in A BRITISH OFFICER! a *veteran* too, as the commander of a packet is always considered! will almost stagger credulity itself. It is, nevertheless, a fact in the present instance; and what is more, the excuse of *stratagem* cannot be made, with effect — for the privateer hailed, demanded the boat, was refused, fired, and gained possession! The mail, however, was previously sunk. — Capt. Bird, T. Williams and D. McLachlan, Esquires, (the other passengers in the *Adolphus*,) arrived at Liverpool, in the *Tontine* cartel, on the 23d of September; as did also Capt. Boulderson and about 150 other persons.[167]

Why did Captain Boulderson sink the mail and strike his colours to an American privateer without resisting? His defence was that he did not know that hostilities had commenced. However in a later legal case it was noted that 'at more than one of the West India Islands the Commander had received an intimation if not actual intelligence to this effect and had issued orders to his Officers and Men accordingly'. But even had he not known,

> it was his Duty when the Privateer was the Aggressor to have defended himself and particularly as he was entrusted with the Mails and Dispatches of the Country his instructions respecting which were to defend them to the utmost that which he ought to have done, even under a total Ignorance of the Circumstances he was highly Criminal in neglecting to do having received intimation that such an event was Extremely probable.[168]

In the American press, it was noted that he was the gentleman who had fired on Washington Morton off Sandy Hook. Maybe the memory of that encounter made him over-cautious; perhaps he also had in mind the time in 1798 when the *Prince Adolphus* was captured under his father's command, and ransomed. If so, it was a disastrous misreading of the political weather. In 1798 the war was with the French, at that point just another episode in the long, intimate and chequered relationship between two old European powers. The individuals concerned felt no great animosity towards one another and it was largely a business matter. In 1812 the United States still had unfinished political business with the colonial power they had driven out, which seemed not to have abandoned its proprietorial attitude. American privateering against the British was a patriotic endeavour.

The consequence for Boulderson of his decision not to resist capture was severe: he was dismissed from the service. The procedure was a formally established one. A committee of 12 Falmouth packet captains assembled in January 1813 to enquire into the circumstances of the capture and Captain Boulderson's conduct. They examined the surgeon, mate, boatswain, carpenter, gunner and seamen of the *Prince Adolphus* who were on board at the time; the master was absent. They also heard the captain's written defence.

The committee sat for five days, after which they reported that they were 'unanimously of opinion that Captain Boulderson is highly reprehensible in not having his Men quartered and Exercised at the great Guns and small Arms' and that 'Captain Boulderson was not justified in sinking the Mail and striking the Colours to the American Privateer without defending the Ship and His Majestys Mails entrusted to his Charge.'[169]

Nonetheless the captains appended a plea for leniency, offering their view that his failure arose from misjudgement rather than cowardice. They would have been very conscious of the likely outcome of their ruling upon one of their fellow-captains.

> At the same time the Committee beg leave to Express their Opinion that Captain Bouldersons Conduct was not actuated by fear or from want of personal Courage but from an Error in Judgment respecting an actual declaration of War with the United States of America for which reason and the long Services of Captain Boulderson his Father and Grand Father before him together with Captain Bouldersons young and large Family this Committee are induced humbly to recommend him to the favorable Consideration of His Majestys Postmaster General.[170]

An American privateer schooner and other vessels near a harbour, c. 1815.
[National Maritime Museum, Greenwich]

Misjudgement it may have been, although the picture we get is of a man frozen by indecision – if not simple dread. Either way, it amounts to a critical flaw in a ship's captain, who at sea cannot pass decisions upwards. The postmaster general did not choose to be lenient.

The loss of the packet was a financial blow to his father. Several years later the matter was revisited, when the elder Boulderson made a claim against the Post Office as joint owner of the captured *Prince Adolphus*, to be compensated for its loss. After the *Earl of Halifax* was taken in 1779 after a long fight, the Post Office had paid him the valuation. In 1798 when the *Prince Adolphus* was captured by a French privateer, he had chosen not to fight, which turned out equally well for him because the government agreed to indemnify those who had paid the ransom. Perhaps that was why he thought it was worth a shot this time too, but it was a long one.

In 1815 he made the first of several applications for compensation to be paid to himself and the other owner (the executors of Robert Lea Jones), and at some point got an opinion from a Mr Maryat, probably Joseph Marryat, a marine underwriter and chairman of Lloyd's. The case hinged on whether the Post Office had a contract with the packet's owner (John Boulderson II) or the commander (John Boulderson III). In 1820 the postmaster general obtained the legal opinion of the attorney general and the solicitor general; they concluded, inevitably, that the contractor was the commander, who could have no claim, regardless of whether the loss resulted from his cowardice or from his culpable mismanagement or negligence.[171] The Post Office declined to pay. John Boulderson II appears to have left no will, possibly because he died without assets.

After his dismissal there is barely another trace of John Boulderson III. In January 1813 he and Mary Anne had four children living, all under the age of seven; there would be five more. In 1819, following the Peterloo Massacre in Manchester (in which troops attacked a large and festive crowd assembled to call for political reform, killing between 10 and 20 people and injuring hundreds), he and his father were among 119 signatories in Cornwall to a loyal declaration in support of the government and against parliamentary reform. John Boulderson II died in 1831 at the age of 82, 'for many years a commander in the packet service and one of the younger brethren of the Trinity Board', noted the *Cornwall Gazette*.

After that there is one more sighting of the third John Boulderson, at a Conservative party dinner along with several other captains. He died in 1838, aged 58 – a young age in that family at least. His grandmother Katherine, widow of John Philips Boulderson, who began her married life in Limehouse, lived to the age of 97. She makes an appearance in a survey of Cornwall published in 1819: 'Boswarran is a neat modern built house, the residence of Mrs. Boulderson'.[172]

John Boulderson III left all he owned to his wife Mary Anne; it was probably not much. Their eldest child, John Carne Boulderson, born in 1806, did not become a seafarer. When he was 16 the Post Office packet service was taken over by the Admiralty, but by then the family inheritance of service on the packets had already been broken. At this point, however, Joseph Boulderson of the East India Company reappears to rescue his brother's family fortunes. By the time of his sudden death in 1828 Joseph had accumulated significant assets, from his marriage settlement and also no doubt from the proceeds of his private adventures over six East India and China voyages. He was a part-owner, at the least, of his late father John's house at Boswarren, his brother John's at Bareppa and other family property near Falmouth. He left all of that to his own four children, but before he died he fixed up solid East India Company careers for at least two of his unfortunate nephew's sons.[173]

A postscript of sorts to the history of the *Prince Adolphus* appeared years later in the *Liverpool Advertiser*:

Sir, Having observed in your last paper notice of a Patent for Sheathing Copper which is to last 15 years, allow me to inform you that I once knew a ship in the packet service, on the Falmouth station, that, when captured by the enemy, had run her copper upward of* ten years: upon making inquiry I was informed that the copper had been laid upon a coat of white paint. — Whether paint agrees better with copper than tar might be easily tried by coppering the two sides of the same ship in the different ways; but my own opinion is, that unalloyed copper would wear as long as it would be expedient to let it remain on. For reference I enclose you the name of the ship and managing owner, and you are at liberty to make any use of this communication you think proper for public benefit. I am, yours, Nauticus.

*Thirteen years was the time stated to me.

Ship Prince Adolphus, Captain Boulderson; Managing Owners, Messrs. Richard Carne & Sons, Falmouth.[174]

Captain Boulderson might perhaps have discussed copper sheathing techniques with Nauticus during the voyage home from Philadelphia in 1812 on board the American cartel, or afterwards in a Liverpool coffee house, waiting for a passage home to Falmouth.

Edward Bamfylde Eagles (1783–1865), *Merchant Brig off Falmouth* [National Maritime Museum, Greenwich]. Eagles served as a lieutenant of marines from 1807, although this study was probably completed much later.

The view from here

As these three packet commanders were in government service, and carried dispatches and news along with mail, a fair picture of their working lives can be put together from documents and newspapers of the time. But they left no diaries or memoirs, and so somewhere near the centre of our field of view there is an empty space.

One eye-witness who can do something to fill in the gaps is Samuel Kelly, already encountered above. He knew both the second John Boulderson and his brother Joseph. Kelly started as a boy on the Falmouth packets before transferring to a troop transport and then to merchant vessels, eventually becoming a merchant captain. After he retired from the sea he wrote an account of his experiences, much of it evidently drawn from his logs or journals. He has bouts of self-righteousness, but he is interested in everything he encounters and writes about the domestic minutiae of maritime life as well as natural curiosities, dramatic events and the occasional flight of fancy.[175]

On a passage to Philadelphia, he knows they are nearing the Newfoundland Banks when the sea is covered with feathers; they see a white butterfly and catch a woodpecker with long yellow legs and a green breast like a parrot. In 1790 near Philadelphia he sees a very long steamboat with paddles under each quarter, stemming the tide at four miles an hour. In Florida the ship's master lays in a few slops to sell to his crew, and each man is supplied with a pair of red baize trousers so that when they are aloft reefing the sails they appear like a flock of flamingoes. When the *Grenville* is captured in 1782 Kelly has some valuable watches from the master's adventure tied up in his shirt-tail to hide them from the Americans, but he is incommoded by them and is glad to be relieved of them when the *Grenville* is retaken by HMS *Garland*, whose people take what they want from the packet.

In Plymouth he notes that women there frequently ply in boats as watermen, which he believes scarcely happens elsewhere. In Deptford when he goes on board the transport *Jason* of Sunderland to sign articles, he finds only the captain's wife and sister there ironing laundry. The 'female captain' pronounces him no sailor since he has not served an apprenticeship in the coal trade. At Leith market on the Firth of Forth a woman selling him greens tells him a pennyworth of spinach is better than two pennyworth of green kale (a fair point). At sea he has a shipmate comb and tie his hair for him, and is cursed by the master for causing the wind to turn against them by combing his hair in the night (this suggests some anxiety on the part of the master involving mermaids).

In 1783 with winter fast approaching, the *Jason* is on the coast of Novia Scotia carrying troops and loyalist emigrants evacuated from Staten Island. The weather being very cold and severe, they land the people with their goods wherever they ask. An old couple with two daughters wish to be landed one afternoon and cannot be persuaded to wait for the next morning, so they are put on shore under a cliff with their furniture about them for shelter. They are still there in the morning and Kelly sees that the tide has been up over them in the night. He goes onshore with a lad and a rope and they haul the belongings to the top of the cliffs, then place them in a circle round the family to protect them from the wind. Kelly is offered an option to remain there as a settler himself, but winter comes on suddenly with sleet and snow settling in large masses on the yards and sails, and his interest in the idea fades.

While Kelly is mate on a merchant brig, a seaman who was on the slave ships gives him such an account of the iniquity practised in the slave trade that he resolves never to go into that work. In 1795, after sailing from Port au Prince to Jamaica with 'two French mulatto women and a negress' as his passengers, in Kingston harbour he finds himself surrounded by slave ships from Africa, the stench from which is intolerable and the noise very unpleasant. Most of the ships in harbour have yellow fever on board. He removes his ship upwind of these vessels but has nothing further to say on the business, bar an observation that the magistrates should employ the negroes of the workhouse to remove the filth accumulating on the wharves and street entrances next to the sea.

He attends the Baptist meeting in Kingston, where the minister, Mr Lyle, is black and there are free black families in the congregation. One Sunday Kelly and two other shipmasters take pleasure, he wants us to know, in preventing several drunken young men from riding their horses into the church. He is told there is a trap-door near the pulpit for escape in case of assault by drunken white inhabitants.[176]

In 1790 he gets command of a leaky old ship and endures a four-month-long winter passage from Liverpool to New York. There is a desperate blow-by-blow narrative of seven weeks battling through almost constant storms and hurricanes. At one point when they were lying to, 'a sea struck the vessel fore and aft her whole length, which shattered the channel bends, broke the remaining rough tree and its stanchions, threw the boats again across the deck and stove the long-boat (the second time), split the covering board of the gunwale, broke the larboard gallows stanchion and two stanchions on the quarter deck, and opened several seams'. He is anxious about their cargo of salt, 'for if the water had got to it, it would have melted and the vessel would have overset'. The broken timber serves as firewood for cooking, but he must reduce the bread rations yet again. Later, when he sees streams of weeds in the water and catches the scent of pine trees on the wind he is confident they are near the continent, although it will be another eleven days before they see Long Island.

Crosbie Garstin, the author who edited Kelly's memoir for publication in 1925, wrote of him: 'he saw history making in his day, the British evacuation of New York; the foundation of St John's, New Brunswick; Benjamin Franklin walking the streets of Philadelphia, a gold chain round his neck; Washington, in black velvet, addressing the Senate'.

Unlike the Boulderson packet captains, Kelly saw no sea battles, but he sailed the same routes and anchored in the same ports as they did, through the same times. The world he describes was also theirs.

Wenceslaus Hollar, *Ships in a storm*, 1627-36. [Rijksmuseum, Amsterdam]

ABBREVIATIONS

With the exception of three archives, and of some individuals whose names occur repeatedly in letters cited, sources in the notes are given in full at first mention and also thereafter unless they follow closely.

Archives

BL	British Library, London
RMA	Royal Mail Archive, British Postal Museum and Archive, London
TNA	The National Archives, Kew, London

Individuals

Bennott	John Burnett Bennott, Post Office inspector of packets
Calder	Admiral Sir Robert Calder, commander-in-chief, Royal Navy, Plymouth
Carne, John	Falmouth merchant and East India Company agent
Chichester	Thomas Pelham, second Earl of Chichester, joint Postmaster General
Croker	John Wilson Croker, first secretary to the Admiralty
Freeling	Francis Freeling, secretary, General Post Office (1798–1836)
Gay	William Gay, deputy to Post Office packet agent at Falmouth
Pender	Benjamin Pender, Post Office packet agent at Falmouth (1785–1810)
Perceval	Spencer Perceval, Prime Minister
PMG	His Majesty's Postmaster General (two individuals jointly during this period)
Sandwich	John Montagu, fifth Earl of Sandwich, joint Postmaster General
Saverland	Christopher Saverland, Post Office packet agent at Falmouth (from 9 May 1810)
Slade	Captain James Slade, senior Royal Navy officer at Falmouth
Todd	Anthony Todd, secretary, General Post Office (1762–65, 1768–98)

NOTES

1 Freeling, 'Desultory observations', 11 Nov 1810. RMA, POST 29/1.
2 John Flavel, *Navigation spiritualiz'd: or, A new compass for seamen* [1682], in *The whole works of the Rev. Mr. John Flavel*, 4th edn, vol. 2, London 1740, pp. 312, 310.
3 Mary Wollstonecraft, *A vindication of the rights of woman*, 1792, Introduction.
4 *The Gentleman's Magazine*, vol. 14, p. 103, 9 Feb 1744; *Caledonian Mercury*, 21 Feb 1744, p. 2.
5 *Proceedings and Acts of the Maryland General Assembly, 1745-1747*, vol. 44, pp. 194-95. On 20 November 1744, in Maryland, Jerningham Bigg published his new wartime tobacco freight rate of £12 per ton, shipping from his anchorage in Herring Bay [John M Hemphill II, 'Freight rates in the Maryland tobacco trade, 1705-1762: Appendix', *Maryland Historical Magazine*, vol. 54, no. 2, Jun 1959, pp. 178-79].
6 *The General Advertiser*, no. 3312, London, 27 Jun 1745, p. 1. The correspondent in Ostend wrote on 5 July NS; a report to the Admiralty from Ostend was dated 4 July. These are New Style dates; unlike the rest of Europe Britain did not adopt the New Style or Gregorian calendar until 1752, hence the apparent discrepancy.
7 *The General Advertiser*, no. 3312, London, 27 Jun 1745, p. 1.
8 *The General Advertiser*, 27 Jun 1745, p. 1.
9 So described by Thomas Powell of Deal in his account of an appeal to the Crown by a Deal parish committee in December 1698, that the town be incorporated as a borough and market town and not subject to the jurisdiction and control of Sandwich; quoted in Stephen Pritchard, *The history of Deal*, 1864, p. 146.
10 William Camden, *Britannia*, trans. Philémon Holland, 1610.
11 Daniel Defoe, *The storm*, 1704; Pritchard, *The history of Deal*, pp. 173-76.
12 Brian Austen, *English provincial posts 1633-1840*, London and Chichester 1978, pp. 1-4, 7-9, 44.
13 On 2 May 1678 the Deal postmaster Morgan Lodge wrote to the Admiralty chasing payment; he had been writing the lists for three years but received no satisfaction [TNA, ADM 106/336/611].
14 Joshua Johnson to John Davidson, 22 Jul 1771. *Joshua Johnson's letterbook 1771-1774: Letters from a merchant in London to his partners*

in Maryland, ed. Jacob M Price, London 1979. Zachariah Hood had formerly been the British tax collector in Maryland.

15 John Marriott, *Beyond the Tower: a history of East London*, 2011, p. 52.

16 John Strype, *A survey of the Cities of London and Westminster*, 1720, II.iv.2, p. 47.

17 The Huguenot cartographer John Rocque (d. 1762) began his survey of London in 1737; it was published in 1746 in a 24-sheet plan engraved by John Pine. A coloured print of a 16-sheet plan based on it, published by Rocque's widow Mary Ann in 1766, is in the Museum of London's collection.

18 Among possible candidates as Joseph's parents are Captain John Baddison or Baldison of Ratcliff and his wife Elizabeth, who in 1680 named a son Joseph, although that particular child died in infancy. Benjamin Bolderston the Southwark shipwright is spelled thus in his will written in 1688, and elsewhere he is variously Baulderstone, Ballderstone, Balderson, Bolderstone and Bolderson; he was probably born in America. He terms himself a 'Shipwright now going on a voyage to Sea in the Merchant Ship Maynard Capt. Robert Gold Commander', and his wife Mary is sole beneficiary. The will was proved in 1692; he may have died in the Battle of Barfleur on board HMS *Essex*, on which his wife's brother Peter Fleming, another shipwright, had served.

19 Judith Boulderson in her will gave the name of her late husband Peter's sister as Elizabeth Phillips; the latter was probably the child of William and Joanna Boulderson who was baptised Elizabeth at Holy Trinity Minories in 1680, and also the Elizabeth Bolderson of Boston who married Joseph Phillips 'of Gt Brittain' in Boston in 1719. There are grounds for supposing that John Philips Boulderson's mother Margaret Philips was related to this Joseph Phillips.

20 Later transcriptions of the Boston First Church records assumed that the unnamed child was James Boulderson, subsequently of Charlestown, Massachusetts, but the latter was most probably James the son of William Boulderson with his first wife Mary, baptised in Canterbury in 1675. A merchant captain named John Balston or Balstone, belonging to a family of Boston shipwrights, may also have been related. He had a house in Water Street, Boston, which was purchased by the First Church in about 1709, sometime after his death, 'the Sellers standing in present need of their money, some of them being bound to sea' [*The records of the First Church in Boston 1630–1868*,

ed. Richard D Pierce, vol. 1, 1961, pp. 121–22, *Electronic texts in American studies*, 62].

21 Possibly Gibson's free school (by then the Coopers' Company school) in School House Lane, Ratcliff, or more likely the Ratcliff Hamlet (later Greencoat) school in White Horse Street. The latter was founded in 1710 and added a girls' school in 1723; its subscribers included numerous sea captains. It also clothed its children and might pay for their apprenticeships, although only up to £3 [Tower Hamlets Archives, London, I/HRS/1, I/HRS/9/1].

22 John Boulderson was bound to Thomas Barnes on 15 November 1733 [Guildhall Library, London Metropolitan Archives, CLC/L/WA/C/020/MS06289/007, fol. 353r]. The merchant Samuel Hyde was a member of the Stepney Society.

23 *The rules and orders of the Stepney Society, with a list of the stewards, from 1674, to 1760*, London 1759, p. 14.

24 The Company of Watermen and Lightermen was a London guild with powers to license watermen and (from 1700) lightermen to work anywhere on the river. Since it was not a city livery company its members were not protected from impressment. According to company records John Boulderson was made free on 11 March 1742/3 [Guildhall Library, London Metropolitan Archives, CLC/L/WA/C/020/MS06289/007, fol. 353r].

25 Katherine Smith's name was usually spelled with an initial C by clerks, with the fifth letter variable. A daughter and granddaughter were also given the name, so for clarity I have spelled this Katherine with a K, since that is how her name appears in the probate register. Her granddaughter who witnessed her will is there named Catherine.

26 The ramifications of this maritime Smith family are hard to follow, not least because of their repeating forenames.

27 Report dated London, 19 Jan 1759, *Oxford Journal*, 20 Jan 1759, p. 3. He would have had to ride by day and much of the night for perhaps three days to cover the 270-odd miles of bad winter roads from Falmouth to London, to match the post boys. The date he came in to Falmouth is not known; the issues of *Lloyd's List* for that year are lost.

28 RMA, Post Office appointment books, POST 58/1, 19 Jan 1759. Robert Rand had himself come to Falmouth from London, sometime after 1753 when he wrote his will in Rotherhithe; one of the witnesses was

a Harwich mariner. He was commissioned with the *Earl of Halifax* in 1757.

29   RMA, POST 58/1, Post Office appointment books, 17 Oct 1755.

30   Supplement to the *New York Mercury*, no. 340, 19 Feb 1759, p. 1. In this and some other reports Captain Morris's vessel was mis-identified as the *Earl of Halifax*. Morris was temporarily dismissed from the service in about May 1757, possibly in connection with events in New York where the *Earl of Halifax* remained for 11 weeks in the winter of 1756–57, before sailing for Falmouth on 13 March (apparently with Benjamin Franklin's stores on board although not the man himself, who postponed his passage). The British military commander Lord Loudon had closed the port to outbound vessels, and the next three packet boats were held there until June 1757.

31   London, February 26, *Leeds Intelligencer*, no. 358, 3 Mar 1761, p. 2.

32   Lodge of Love and Honour, Falmouth [Library and Museum of Freemasonry, London, Register of Admissions: Country and Foreign, vol II, fol. 45]. John Boulderson's firing glass is illustrated in Percy Bate, 'Old English glasses', *The Studio*, 15 Oct 1901, and again in Bate's *English table glass*, London and New York [1905], facing p. 112, no. 234. It was said by Bate to belong to Major Francis Walter Allan, a Glasgow freemason who died in 1918, but I do not know where it is now.

33   *The London Evening-Post* no. 5659, 9 Feb 1764, p. 1. A list of bankrupts printed in *The Gentleman's Magazine* of May 1765 [vol. 35, p. 248] includes Henry Bird and Joseph Quallet of Rotherhithe, shipwrights, although the ship builders Bird and Quallet at Pitch house Point, Rotherhithe, are listed in trade directories from 1768 to 1770. Pitch House or Pitchers Point was across the river from Shadwell, and there were shipwrights named Quallet living in Shadwell when John Philips Boulderson was growing up there.

34   *Pennsylvania Gazette*, no. 1851, 14 Jun 1764, p. 2.

35   New-York, Feb. 28. *Boston Evening-Post*, no. 1540, 11 Mar 1765, p. 2.

36   *Ipswich Journal*, 1 Dec 1764, p. 2; *Oxford Journal*, 5 Jan 1765, p. 3. The *Earl of Halifax* sailed from Falmouth in the middle of December 1764.

37   *The Montresor journals*, ed. G D Scull, New York 1882, pp. 352–53.

38   John Flavel, *Divine conduct: or, The mystery of Providence opened* [1678], in *The whole works of the Rev. Mr. John Flavel*, 4th edn, vol. 2, London 1740, p. 159.

39 Susan Gay, *Old Falmouth*, London 1903, p. 146. Susan Gay (1845–1918) was the granddaughter of the last Post Office packet agent at Falmouth, William Gay; she visited there in childhood and later lived nearby. She does not specify which of the Bouldersons lived in Mulberry Square, or when; it was probably something she heard in her youth. Mulberry Square was the location of the Custom House until 1785.

40 Henry Laurens to John Hopton, New York, 4 Sep 1771; Henry Laurens to Joseph Wharton Jr, New York, 7 Sep 1771; Henry Laurens to James Laurens, Halifax Packet, 9 Sep 1771. *The papers of Henry Laurens, volume seven, August 1, 1769 to October 9, 1771*, Columbia, SC, 1979, pp. 558, 570, 583.

41 Henry Laurens to William Fisher, Falmouth, 12 Oct 1771. *The papers of Henry Laurens, volume eight, October 10, 1771 to April 19, 1773*, Columbia, SC, 1980, pp. 7, 8.

42 Henry Laurens to Samuel Groube, Westminster, 4 Apr 1772. *The papers of Henry Laurens: volume eight*, pp. 244–46.

43 Henry Laurens to George Appleby, Westminster, 28 Feb and 10 Mar 1774. *The papers of Henry Laurens: volume nine, April 19, 1773 to December 12, 1774*, Columbia, SC, 1981, pp. 316–18, 347.

44 Edward Lawrance's Packet journal, 16 Jun 1776. 'Memorandum written on a Voyage from Falmo. to Madeira, the West India Islands & back again to Falmouth in the Anna Teresa packet Boat. by E.L.', National Maritime Museum Cornwall [transcript, https://www.maritimeviews.co.uk/edward-lawrances-journal/]

45 *Samuel Kelly: an eighteenth century seaman*, ed. Crosbie Gartin, London 1925, pp. 50, 58–59. Joseph Boulderson was then sailing-master on his brother's packet, the *Earl of Halifax*, but at Charleston in April 1782 he transferred with some of its crew to the *Grenville* packet after the latter had been taken by an American privateer and then recaptured by a British navy vessel, to bring the vessel back to Falmouth. Kelly's 'Captain B' appears to have been Joseph rather than John Boulderson since the *Earl of Halifax* reached Falmouth in June and sailed again for New York on 20 July 1782, while the *Grenville* did not reach Plymouth from Charleston until 8 August, according to *Lloyd's List*. But the picture is not entirely clear: the *Earl of Halifax*'s captain on the July sailing is not named and may have been another master, while Kelly thought the *Grenville* got back from Charleston in early July, and in any case he bore a grudge against both Bouldersons.

46   *American Archives*, ed. Peter Force, 4th series, vol. 2, Washington 1839, 1304.

47   *American Archives*, 4th series, vol. 2, 1017.

48   *Providence Gazette*, 24 Jun 1775, p. 3.

49   *Pennsylvania Evening Post*, 1 Jul 1775, p. 277.

50   *American Archives*, 4th series, vol. 2, 985.

51   *London Evening Post*, 30 May to 1 Jun 1775, p. 2; *Derby Mercury*, 26 May to 2 Jun 1775, p. 3; *American Archives*, 4th series, vol. 2, 298; *Diary and letters of Thomas Hutchinson*, vol. 1, Boston 1884, pp. 455, 464, 466. Franklin was on his way back to Philadelphia when the news reached Whitehall; the depositions were placed in the charge of the radical John Wilkes, who happened at the time to be lord mayor of London.

52   *Oxford Journal*, no. 1162, 5 Aug 1775, p. 2.

53   Lord Dartmouth to Governor Sir Guy Carleton, Whitehall, 2 Aug 1775. *The Manuscripts of the Earl of Dartmouth*, vol. 2, *Historical Manuscripts Commission, 11th Report, appendix, pt 5*, 1895, p. 344.

54   William Tryon to Whitehead Hicks, 19 Oct 1775. *American Archives*, 4th series, vol. 3, Washington 1840, 1054.

55   William Tryon to the Earl of Dartmouth, 11 Nov 1775. *Documents relative to the colonial history of the state of New York*, vol. 8, New York 1853, p. 643.

56   L H Butterfield, 'The milliner's mission in 1775', *The William and Mary Quarterly*, third series, vol. 8, no. 2, Apr 1951, p. 194.

57   L H Butterfield, 'The milliner's mission', p. 195.

58   John Boulderson to Todd, 16 Dec 1775. 'George III: December 1775', *Calendar of Home Office Papers (George III): 1773-5*, ed. Richard Arthur Roberts, London 1899, p. 501.

59   L H Butterfield, 'The milliner's mission', pp. 197-99.

60   L H Butterfield, 'The milliner's mission', p. 196.

61   Henry Jeffery to Todd, *Lord Hyde*, Boston, 16 Jan 1776. TNA, CO 5/135, fol. 90. He sent the letter by the *Julius Caesar* for London, which made Plymouth on 11 February.

62   Henry Jeffery to Todd, *Lord Hyde*, Boston, 31 Jan 1776. TNA, CO 5/135, fols 97-98. He sent this letter by the *Canceau* armed cutter which arrived at Spithead on 23 February.

63   *Derby Mercury*, 3 May 1776, pp. 2, 3; *Diary and letters of Thomas Hutchinson*, vol. 2, 1884, pp. 42-43, 46-48. The newspaper printed an account of the retreat from Boston supplied by one of Howe's officers

now in London (unnamed but probably Colonel Browne who came over on the *Lord Hyde*). This officer wrote that the general had received no information from England since 16 October 1775, which was the day the *Lord Hyde* sailed from Falmouth.

64 Extract from the journal of Chief Justice Peter Oliver, *Diary and letters of Thomas Hutchinson*, vol. 2, 1884, p. 53.

65 Olaudah Equiano, *The interesting narrative of the life of Olaudah Equiano, or Gustavus Vassa, the African, written by himself*, ed. Brycchan Carey, Oxford 2018. The book was first published *c.* 1789. Equiano writes that he was born in Essaka, Eboe, in Guinea (now part of Nigeria); however a parish record of his baptism in St Margaret's Westminster at the age of 12 gives his birthplace as Carolina, as does one later record. For what it's worth, my view is that neither memoirs nor retrospectively-compiled birthplace data can be altogether relied upon.

66 'Extract of a letter from a Gentleman who has escaped from the Provincials at New-York, and joined the army under General Howe, Staten Island, Aug. 17', *Manchester Mercury*, 7 Oct 1776, p. 5.

67 The *Derby Mercury* of 18 October reported rumours that New York was taken. A Bristol merchant ship heading home from Jamaica, the *Hanover Planter*, fell in with the *Galatea*, a British man of war hunting privateers in the western Atlantic, on 23 September (three days before the *Earl of Halifax* left New York), and reached Bristol on 23 October. The navy captain's account of the capture of the city was in the British newspapers by the end of October, including the *Caledonian Mercury* [30 Oct 1776, p. 2] and *Stamford Mercury* [31 Oct 1776, p. 2]. General Howe's dispatches dated 21 and 23 September were sent by the *Earl of Halifax* and received in London on 2 November [*The Public Hue-and-Cry*, no. 63, 8 Nov 1776, p. 2].

68 Hugh Finlay to Todd, Quebec, 30 May 1777. TNA, CO 5/136, fol. 54.

69 Todd to William Knox, GPO, 2 Dec 1778. TNA, CO 5/136, fols 192–93.

70 Stephen Bell to Todd, Falmouth, 14 Feb 1778 (copy). TNA, CO 5/136, fol. 87r.

71 Stephen Bell to Todd, Falmouth, 14 Feb 1778 (copy). TNA, CO 5/136, fol. 87v.

72 John Boulderson to Todd, Falmouth, 14 Feb 1778. TNA, CO 5/136, fol. 89.

73 That Mary Williams was 'of St Helena' is known only from brief family notes made by her great-great-grandson George Boulderson

(1889–1969); other information he noted about his 18th-century forebears is verifiably correct. A Mary Williams was paid £25 by the St Helena vestry in 1756 for nursing an elderly woman. One of the departing loyalists was Samuel Carne of Charleston, who before returning to London had first in 1776 retreated to the country place of a Mr Williams, possibly the attorney Robert Williams who had a Beaufort County plantation, or John Williams, later of Arundell Street in the Strand, London, who was named in Samuel Carne's will. It seems most likely that Mary Williams was from South Carolina. (Cornwall has no parish of St Helena; there is however a small stone house named St Helena or Elena in the parish of Landewednack south of Falmouth, which appears to date from the eighteenth century or earlier and may once have belonged to a mariner.)

74 'London, Nov. 19. The Halifax packet, which sailed the 12th of July from Jamaica, has never been heard of. She mounted 20 guns, and was reckoned a very prime sailer.' [*Bath Chronicle and Weekly Gazette*, 25 Nov 1779, p. 1].

75 *Lloyd's List*, London, 30 Nov 1779.

76 *Kentish Gazette*, 1 Dec 1779, p. 3. The news was in New York by 6 October [*Pennsylvania Journal, or, Weekly Advertiser*, 27 Oct 1779, pp. 2–3].

77 *Derby Mercury*, 17 Dec 1779, p. 3; Stephen Bell to Todd, Falmouth, 12 and 16 Dec 1779, RMA, POST 48/5.

78 TNA, HCA 26/42, Registers of Declarations for Letters of Marque against France, fol. 153, 12 May 1781.

79 *Samuel Kelly: an eighteenth century seaman*, ed. Crosbie Gartin, London 1925, pp. 45–46.

80 *Samuel Kelly*, pp. 48–49.

81 *Samuel Kelly*, pp. 50, 56.

82 BL, IOR/L/MAR/C/656, Commanders and mates examined by the Committee of Shipping (1794–1798), p. 228. His age is given there as 19, but he was born in January 1779.

83 *The Times*, London, 30 Nov 1797, p. 3. John Philips Boulderson's baptismal second name was from his mother; however in the probate register in 1798 it was spelled Phillips.

84 *Caledonian Mercury*, Edinburgh, 9 Jul 1798, p. 2.

85 John Bullocke to Pender, HMP *Prince Adolphus*, Lisbon, 16 Jun 1798. TNA, T 1/808, Treasury papers.

86 John Bullocke to Pender, HMP *Prince Adolphus*, Lisbon, 16 Jun 1798. TNA, T 1/808.

87 Henry Pigot and others to Robert Walpole, Lisbon, 21 Jun 1798 (copy). TNA, T 1/808.

88 Henry Pigot and others to Robert Walpole and Walpole's reply, both Lisbon, 21 Jun 1798 (copies); Thomas Gonne to Freeling, Lisbon, 23 Jun 1798. TNA, T 1/808.

89 PMG to Lords Commissioners of the Treasury, 8 Jul 1798. TNA, T 1/808.

90 Thomas Gonne to Freeling, Lisbon, 23 Jun 1798. TNA, T 1/808.

91 PMG to Lords Commissioners of the Treasury, 8 Jul 1798. TNA, T 1/808.

92 PMG to Lords Commissioners of the Treasury, 25 Sep 1798. TNA, T 1/811.

93 Extract of a letter from Thomas Gonne to Freeling, 5 Sep 1798, encl. in PMG to Treasury Commissioners, 25 Sep 1798. TNA, T 1/811.

94 TNA, ADM 103/468, ADM 103/476, ADM 103/506.

95 RMA, POST 74/713, Case as to the Prince Adolphus packet, fol. 4.

96 Edward Lawrance, 'Memorandum written on a Voyage from Falmo. to Madeira, the West India Islands & back again to Falmouth in the Anna Teresa packet Boat. by E.L.', Bartlett Library, National Maritime Museum Cornwall [transcription at https://www.maritimeviews.co.uk/edward-lawrances-journal/].

97 BL, IOR/L/MAR/C/656, Commanders and mates examined by the Committee of Shipping (1794–1798), p. 228. This document has him making two New York voyages as a seaman, which could be what he told the EIC, having added two years to his age; however during the period in question the *Earl of Halifax* only sailed to New York once in 1789 when he was 10, and once in 1792 when he was 13, otherwise taking the West India route. He may well have been on board as a 10-year-old, but to call him a seaman then would be stretching the point.

98 BL, IOR/L/MAR/B/373C, Journal of the 3rd voyage of the *Marquis of Lansdown*.

99 BL, IOR/L/MAR/B/373C, Journal of the 3rd voyage of the *Marquis of Lansdown*, IOR/L/MAR/C/656, Description of commanders and mates examined by the Committee of Shipping 1794–1798. The *Marquis of Lansdown* left Brunswick dock at Blackwall in March 1793, but

midshipman Boulderson may have boarded a month later at Gravesend with his uncle, about two weeks after the impress boat was fought off.

100 Bennott to Freeling, Plymouth, 6 Nov 1800. RMA, POST 43/135, Reports by the Inspector of Packets. The inspector's last name was written Bennett or Bennet by absolutely everybody at the time except himself, including the clerk who transcribed his will into the probate register. He even did so himself on his marriage certificate in 1782, but under his Post Office reports and minutes his autograph signature, John Burnett Bennott, is unmistakable.

101 Extract of a letter Freeling to Pender, 25 Nov 1800. RMA, POST 43/135.

102 Gay to Freeling, Falmouth, 3 Dec 1800. RMA, POST 43/135.

103 [Freeling], cover minute to PMG on Bennott's report of 8 Dec 1800; Freeling to Pender, 6 Dec 1800 (copy). RMA, POST 43/135.

104 PMG to Treasury Commissioners, 29 Sep 1802. RMA, POST 1/20, Treasury letters, 26. The bill of sale contains a description of the *Earl of Halifax*: 'in a Certificate under the Hands of John Symons and Robert Symons the Builders dated the 27th October One thousand Eight hundred, and never before registered and John Whitter Tide Surveyor having certified unto us that the said Ship or Vessel is British built has two Decks and three Masts, that her length from the fore Part of the Main Stem to the after part of the Tafrel aloft is Eighty Six Feet her Breadth at the broadest Part, above the Main Wales Twenty three feet and nine inches her Height between Decks under Beams, five feet three inches and half inch and admeasures One hundred and Eighty five & 72/94 Tons; that she is a Square Sterned Ship has no Gallery and a Scroll Head' [RMA, POST 43/214].

105 *Cornwall Gazette and Falmouth Packet*, Falmouth, 21 Aug 1802.

106 Notice dated Falmouth, 23 Aug 1802, *Cornwall Gazette and Falmouth Packet*, 28 Aug 1802, p. 2.

107 *Cornwall Gazette and Falmouth Packet*, 28 Aug 1802, p. 3. The *Duke of Cumberland* was bought in by the Post Office on 25 June 1803 from the joint owners, John Boulderson the elder and John Jones Junior as executor of his father Robert Lea Jones [RMA, POST 43/214]. In a memorandum added to his will shortly before his death, Robert Lea Jones instructed that his half share in the *Prince Adolphus* be sold to pay for his bequests. Post Office correspondence with the Treasury in 1802 regarding the valuation of the *Duke of Cumberland* does not distinguish between the elder Boulderson, who was part-owner, and his son who

'introduced her to the service' when he was commissioned; that issue would become central to a legal case ten years later after the loss of the *Prince Adolphus* [RMA, POST 43/135, Packet Inspector's report, 15 Sep 1802].

108 Tony Pawlyn, *The Falmouth packets 1689–1851*, Truro 2003, p. 67.

109 Richard Carne & Sons were master ropemakers in Falmouth. As noted above, the third John Boulderson's parents may well have been acquainted with a South Carolina merchant named Samuel Carne who departed in haste from Charleston in 1777 during the American revolutionary war and disinherited his patriot son, but I can find only the suspicion of a link between the numerous Carnes of Cornwall and Samuel Carne of Charleston and London (1723–1786). Samuel was born in London to Arundell Mauleverer Carne, whose extravagant name may refer to Sir Richard Arundell, a governor of Pendennis castle, or his son Sir John Arundell, MP for Truro, who in 1693 married the widow of Sir Richard Mauleverer.

110 BL, IOR/L/MAR/C/654, Commanders and mates examined by the Committee of Shipping, 1783–1788; *Samuel Kelly: an eighteenth century seaman*, ed. Crosbie Gartin, London 1925, p. 50.

111 *The Monthly Magazine*, vol. 24, part 2, London 1807, p. 305.

112 *A view of the opening of the London Docks Wapping on the 31st January 1805*, engraving after Edward Francis Burney, 1805.

113 Two years later sexual licentiousness at the Wapping dock was lampooned by Thomas Rowlandson after (it is presumed) Henry William Bunbury, in a print entitled *Black Brown & Fair*. The title referred to the choice of ethnicities available to customers of a dockside brothel. The opening of London Dock on 30 January 1805 is described in Joseph Nightingale, *London and Middlesex, or, An historical, commercial, & descriptive survey of the metropolis of Great-Britain*, vol. 3, 1815, p. 145.

114 Arthur William Devis, *Portrait of Captain Joseph Boulderson*, c. 1808–1822, Ferens Art Gallery, Hull.

115 The Hull connection probably began earlier through his wife's family; Morleys in Hull included a timber merchant.

116 Although she outlived him, the sole mention of the former Sarah Morley in Joseph Boulderson's will is oblique. He refers to the sums to which he or any of his children may be entitled under the marriage

settlement in their own right or as administrators or executors or next of kin 'to my wife their Mother'.

117 He was a tenant of the Rugby Estate in the parish of St Andrew Holborn.

118 Shadwell Money Reid Boulderson was born at Patna, India in 1832 and died near Bristol in 1847; he was buried at Kensal Green in London.

119 The sitter is identified as Shadwell Boulderson. The portrait is attributed to James Sant (1820-1916) and is in the collection of Somerset Museums Service. Sant also painted the boy's maternal grandfather Wigram Money (not to be confused with the shipbuilder Money Wigram), who probably had the two portraits done at around the same time, after he retired from the Bengal civil service. Shadwell Money Boulderson died in 1847, his grandfather in 1857; both were buried at Kensal Green. Brislington was a purpose-built private asylum established by Edward Long Fox, a son of the Falmouth surgeon Joseph Fox who in 1766 had set up a house in Falmouth 'for harbouring Sick Seamen' [Susan Gay, *Old Falmouth*, 1903, p. 87]. The boy was a gentleman patient, however the Brislington regime had a reputation among some former inmates for cruelty and degradation.

120 A detailed factual account of the incident, said to have come from someone who went on board the *Chesapeake* the following day, appeared on the front of the *Maryland Herald and Hager's-Town Weekly Advertiser* of 10 July 1807, reprinted from the *Norfolk Ledger* of 24 June 1807. Commentary in the newspaper proposes that since the men were thought to have deserted on 9 or 10 March, and answers to letters written to London as late as 20 March had now been received in Norfolk, Virginia, the admiral in Halifax who issued *Leopard's* orders could have been acting under express instructions from the government in London.

121 Washington Morton's letter dated 20 August 1807 was printed in the New York republican newspaper the *American Citizen*, 21 Aug 1807, p. 2. It was reproduced in the federalist *New York Daily Advertiser*, 24 Aug 1807, p. 2.

122 *American Citizen*, 22 Aug 1807, p. 2; *New York Daily Advertiser*, 24 Aug 1807, p. 2. The story was in the London newspapers by early October.

123 *American Citizen*, 22 Aug 1807, p. 2; *New York Daily Advertiser*, 24 Aug 1807, p. 2.

124 The packet's dates in and out of Halifax do not to my knowledge appear in any marine lists but they are given in John Olenkiewicz's 'British packet sailings Falmouth–North America: 1755–1840', 2013, a database that also draws on philatelic sources [accessible at rfrajola.com in January 2019]. *Prince Adolphus*'s arrival in New York on 20 August was listed in the *New York Evening Post* of 20 August 1807, and Captain Boulderson's marine intelligence appeared in the *New York Daily Advertiser* of 21 August 1807.

125 *American Citizen*, 24 Aug 1807, p. 2.

126 *American Citizen*, 24 Aug 1807, p. 2.

127 Saverland to Freeling, Falmouth, 15 Aug 1810 [RMA, POST 29/1]. One version of the petition is dated 13 August. Saverland was appointed Falmouth packet agent on 9 May 1810; he had followed his father into Post Office service, becoming packet agent at Helvoetsluys in Holland in 1778 at the age of 21; he was later postmaster at Portsmouth and then a Post Office surveyor in Leicestershire; the Post Office paid his removal costs from there to Falmouth.

128 Petition of petty officers and seamen of the Falmouth packets to the Postmaster General, in two versions: one undated, received in the agent's office on 15 August 1810, specifying the wages requested and signed by two men from each of 11 packets; the other, dated 13 August 1810, was in the agent's office on 20 August 1810 and filed in Freeling's office on 27 August 1810, it was unsigned and with no amounts specified. The quotation here is from the latter [RMA, POST 29/1].

129 Saverland to Freeling, Falmouth, 15 Aug 1810. RMA, POST 29/1.

130 Freeling, cover minute to PMG, GPO, 18 Aug 1810. RMA, POST 29/1.

131 Saverland, private letter to Freeling, Falmouth, 20 Aug 1810. RMA, POST 29/1.

132 Freeling, private letter to Saverland, GPO, 20 Aug 1810 (copy). RMA, POST 29/1.

133 Saverland to Freeling, Falmouth, 24 Oct 1810. RMA, POST 29/1.

134 Slade to Croker, HMS *Experiment*, Falmouth, 24 Oct 1810. RMA, POST 29/1.

135 Undated note received in Saverland's office 25 Oct 1810. RMA, POST 29/1.

136 Saverland to Freeling, Falmouth, 25 Oct 1810; Freeling to PMG, Battersea, 28 Oct 1810. RMA, POST 29/1.

137 Saverland to Freeling, Falmouth, 25 Oct 1810. RMA, POST 29/1.

138 Saverland to Calder, Saverland to Freeling, both Falmouth, 26 Oct 1810. RMA, POST 29/1.

139 Saverland to Freeling, Falmouth, 27 Oct 1810. RMA, POST 29/1.

140 Description of the delegates provided by Henry Williams, the searcher, enc. with Saverland to Freeling, Falmouth, 27 Oct 1810 [RMA, POST 29/1]. Sir Francis Burdett was a popular radical politician who had been arrested earlier that year after the House of Commons found him guilty of breach of privilege; he was confined for several weeks in the Tower of London.

141 Tony Pawlyn, *The Falmouth packets 1689-1851*, Truro 2003, pp. 104-05.

142 Slade to Croker, HMS *Experiment*, Falmouth, 28 Oct 1810; Saverland to Freeling, Falmouth, 5 Nov 1810. RMA, POST 29/1.

143 Copy of the Examination of John Parker & Richard Pascoe at the Mansion House, 30 Oct 1810. RMA, POST 29/1. The events in Falmouth coincided with the golden jubilee of the ailing George III.

144 Saverland to Freeling and enc. proclamation, Falmouth, 31 Oct 1810. RMA, POST 29/1.

145 Saverland to Freeling on receipt of his letter of 29 Oct, and private letter to Freeling, both Falmouth, 31 Oct 1810. RMA, POST 29/1.

146 Packet seamen to Saverland, HMS *Experiment,* 31 Oct 1810. RMA, POST 29/1.

147 Saverland to Freeling, Falmouth, 2 Nov 1810. RMA, POST 29/1.

148 Freeling to Saverland, GPO, 31 Oct 1810 (copy). RMA, POST 29/1.

149 Gay to Freeling, Agent's Office, Falmouth, 6 Nov 1810. RMA, POST 29/1.

150 Slade to Croker, HMS *Experiment*, Falmouth, 6 Nov 1810 and 7 Nov 1810. RMA, POST 29/1.

151 Slade to Saverland, HMS *Experiment*, Falmouth, 7 Nov 1810. RMA, POST 29/1.

152 Saverland, private letters to Freeling, Plymouth Dock, 13 Nov and 17 Nov 1810. RMA, POST 29/1.

153 Petition of the packet seamen at Falmouth who were engaged in the mutiny, Falmouth, 23 Nov 1810. RMA, POST 29/1.

154 Walter Callaway to Davies Giddy, Trewinnard, 25 Nov 1810. RMA, POST 29/1.

155 John Callaway to his parents, HMS *L'Aigle*, Plymouth, 27 Nov 1810. RMA, POST 29/1.

156 Saverland, private letter to Freeling, Plymouth Dock, 6 Dec 1810. RMA, POST 29/1.

157 Captain Randlett gave an extensive account of his experiences to a Philadelphia newspaper much later, but he did not provide the date on which the *Swaggerer* arrived with the war news. *Pocahontas* was claimed as a prize and he himself was detained in Suriname; he was not returned to the Unites States until the following summer [*Poulson's American Daily Advertiser*, 13 Sep 1813, p. 2]. The *Columbian Phenix* of Providence, Rhode Island [11 Dec 1813, p. 2] reported the trial in that town of the American sailor William Ross for piracy and murder (a passenger was killed during the hijacking), although the seizure at Cape Verde is dated to 6 August 1812, which is at odds with both Randlett's account and other marine data. Ross was acquitted.

158 The Suriname and Demarara sailings can be dated from July 1812 issues of the *Essequebo & Demerary Royal Gazette*, George-Town. The *Barbados Mercury, and Bridge-town Gazette* of 25 July 1812 states firmly that the packet 'will sail today' [p. 2].

159 *Hope's Philadelphia Price-Current, and Commercial Record*, Philadelphia, 7 Sep 1812, p. 3.

160 The *Cornwall Gazette* of 31 October 1812 reported that the packet had been given up 'without a shot fired' [p. 2]. American newspapers published Captain Lucet's tally of prizes with extracts from his log book; the *American & Commercial Daily Advertiser* of Baltimore, Maryland on 24 August 1812 was among the first. Lucet seized the *Prince Adolphus* in 24 48 N, 63 8 W, thus about 640 nautical miles north-northwest of Martinique, on the expected homeward course. I have found no sailing dates for the *Prince Adolphus* after the packet left Barbados on 25 July, but it was scheduled to call at Martinique and then Guadeloupe before setting sail for Falmouth.

161 *New-Jersey Journal*, Elizabethtown, NJ, 10 Nov 1812, p. 3, reprinted from the *Weekly Aurora*, Philadelphia, of unknown date.

162 *Poulson's American Daily Advertiser*, Philadelphia, 28 Sep 1812, p. 2.

163 *American Advocate*, Maine, 3 Sep 1812, p. 3; *Grotjan's Philadelphia Public-Sale Report*, Philadelphia, 5 Oct 1812, p. 2.

164 *Lloyd's List*, London, 20 Oct 1812; *Morning Chronicle*, London, 30 Oct 1812, p. 3; *Morning Post*, London, 30 Oct 1812, p. 4. Alongside a prisoner exchange list headed 17 August 1812 is a note that Captain Boulderson, his crew and his passengers were released by the Pennsylvania marshal

to the secretary of the British legation to the United States, 'but were not exchanged, as they were sent to England & probably had been exchd there' [TNA, ADM 103/465 (pt 2), American and British prisoners, 1812–1815].

165 *Cornwall Gazette*, Truro, 31 Oct 1812, pp. 2, 3.

166 *Barbados Mercury, and Bridge-town Gazette*, 21 Jul and 25 Jul 1812. The news from Washington had already reached St Bartholomew and then Martinique, possibly via the Leeward Islands navy station on Antigua.

167 *Essequebo and Demerary Royal Gazette*, George-Town, 12 Dec 1812 [National Archive of the Netherlands, NL-HaNA, Dutch Series Guyana, 1.05.21, inv.nr. *AH.3A*]. *Lloyd's List* of 20 October 1812 has the *Tontine* arriving in Liverpool on 17 September.

168 RMA, POST 74/713: Case as to the Prince Adolphus packet, fol. 13.

169 RMA, POST 74/713, fol. 10.

170 RMA, POST 74/713, fol. 10.

171 RMA, POST 74/713, Case as to the Prince Adolphus packet, opinion, Lincoln's Inn, 20 Nov 1820.

172 William Penaluna, *The circle or historical survey of sixty parishes and towns in Cornwall*, Helston 1819, p. 38.

173 BL, IOR/L/MIL/9/150/86; BL, IOR/L/MIL/11/44/197.

174 *Gore's Liverpool General Advertiser*, 2 Oct 1823, p. 4.

175 *Samuel Kelly: an eighteenth century seaman*, ed. Crosbie Garstin, London 1925, *passim*.

176 The Baptist preacher was George Liele, born into slavery in Virginia and freed in Jamaica. Kelly's account of white men trying to ride horses into Liele's meeting house is corroborated by a very similar event at one of Liele's meetings described in the *Baptist Quarterly*, vol. 20, no. 8, Oct 1964, p. 346.

ACKNOWLEDGEMENTS

A long time back, during a visit to the Bartlett research centre at the National Maritime Museum Cornwall in Falmouth (being a typographer who had switched from formatting other people's's words to writing my own), by great good fortune I found myself seated beside the maritime historian Tony Pawlyn. He devoted his entire afternoon to providing a crash course in the use of maritime research material, supplemented by a fat wad of data printouts. Years later when work on the Boulderson packet captains was nearly done I contacted the Bartlett again to check a few points, and it was Tony who answered. With great generosity he undertook to read a draft of the packet captains' story. Needless to say, all mistakes and misrepresentations are mine, but my debt to Tony is immense.

The Royal Mail Archive at the Postal Museum in London holds a collection of early Post Office papers which includes some matchless sources for the history of the packet service. I am most grateful to the archivists there for their endless patience and helpfulness in allowing me to examine and record large bundles of fragile documents. My thanks for help of various kinds are also due to philatelists Richard Frajola and John Olenkiewicz, and to Jessie Serfilippi at the Schuyler Mansion, Albany, New York. I am also indebted to indexer Marian Aird, to Bill Norris of Central Books, and to David Parsons at Imprint Digital in Exeter. Their judicious expertise, sage advice and ready response to pressing requests have been indispensable. Beyond that, I have been sustained by the intellectual levity reliably offered by those who share the space I live in, for which I thank them.

One further debt should be acknowledged here: to generations of long-gone newspaper editors and their numerous correspondents, on both sides of the Atlantic and across more than a century. Their tireless day-by-day reporting of the events of their times, both history-making and incidental, is something to be thankful for, the more so since this is a story about people who carried the news.

INDEX

Devis, Arthur William, *Portrait of Captain Joseph Boulderson (c.1808–1822)*, 69–70, *71*
Diana (ship), 87
disease, on the West Indies route, 67
Dispatch (ship), 87
Dodd, Ralph, 68
Dover, packet service, 16, 25–6
Duchess of Gordon (ship), 38
Duke of Cumberland (ship), 63–6, 116 n107
Duke of Marlborough (ship), 80, 81, 82

Eagles, Edward Bamfylde, *Merchant Brig off Falmouth, 101*
Earl of Halifax (ship): Falmouth to New York packet service, 24–30, 32; ownership of, 34, 54; launch of second packet boat (1764), 28; during the American Revolutionary war, 38–44; Falmouth to West Indies mail service, 45; shipworm, 45–6; launch of third packet boat (1781), 49–50; taken by the American privateer *General Starke*, 48–9; bill of sale, 116 n104
Earl of Leicester (ship), 26
East India Company, 15, 46, 54, 67, 70, 72, 100
Eastwood, Richard, 86
Eller, John, 86
Equiano, Olaudah, 42, 113 n65
Experiment, HMS, 80, 82, 86
Express (ship), 87

Falmouth, Cornwall: overseas mail service, 7, 25, 53, 62; maritime community in, 8; Freemasons' lodge, 27; reputation for fish, 33; Olaudah Equiano's impressions of, 42; *Prince Adolphus* built near, 53; seamen's strike (1810), 78–90, 119 n128
Fenner, Henry, 60, 62
Fittock, John, 86
Flavel, John, 30
Flushing, Cornwall, 53, 81, 82

Fort Duquesne, Battle of (1758), 24
Fort George, Manhattan, 26, *27*
Fort William (ship), 68
Fox, Edward Long, 118 n119
Fox, Joseph, 118 n119
Franklin (ship), 50
Franklin, Benjamin, 37, 41, 104, 110 n30
Freeling, Francis, 57–8, 60, 64, 78–9, 81–7, 90
French and Indian War *see* Seven Years' War
French revolutionary war, 53, 63
fumigation, 67, 88

Gage, General Thomas, 36, 37, 38
Galatea (ship), 113 n67
Garland, HMS, 102
Garstin, Crosbie, 104
Gay, Susan, 111 n39
Gay, William, 64, 87, 111 n39
General Starke (ship), 48
General Wall (ship), 27
George II, King, 10
George III, King, 26, 70, 120 n143
Germain, Lord George, 44
Gibson's Free School, 109 n21
Giddy, Davies, 89
Gillimore, Walter, 85
Gonne, Thomas, 56, 58–9, 60
Goodwin Sands, 14–15
Gordon, Cosmo Percy Boulderson, 72
Gordon, William, 71–2
Governor McKean (ship), 93–4, 95, 96
Great Storm (1703), 16
Grenville (ship), 33, 50–2, 102
Groube, Samuel, 30–1, 32, 39–40
Guyana *see* Demerara (modern Guyana)

Hamilton, Alexander, 76
Hanover Planter (ship), 113 n67
Harlequin (ship), 64
Harriot (ship), 42
Heather, William: *Chart of Plymouth Sound (1798), 91*; *Chart of the entrances to Falmouth and Helford (1798), 65*

American Revolutionary war, 35–8, 44, 113 n67; British Post Office ceases operations in, 41; fire (1776), 44; *Prince Adolphus* and the Washington Morton incident, 73–7; *A view of Fort George with the City of New York* (1736), *27*

New York Gazette, 24

news, conveyance of, 8, 16, 24, 29, 36–7

'no taxation without representation', 28

Nocton (ship), 87, 89

North Star, HMS, 87

Nymph (ship), 94

Oke, William, 86

Oliver, Peter, 42

Orchard, Hanable, 86

Ostend, 12–14

Oxford Journal, 38

packet boats: carriage of passengers, 29, 61; overseas mail service, 7–8; seamen's strike (1810), 78–86; taken over by the Admiralty, 100

Parker, John, 82–5, 87, 90

Pascal, Captain, 42

Pascoe, Michael, 86

Pascoe, Richard, 82–5, 87, 90

Peijrusset, Captain, 56

Pellew, Samuel, 84

Pender, Benjamin, 56, 58, 64

Perceval, Spencer, 89

Peterloo Massacre (1819), 99

Peters, Alexander, 86

Phillips, Elizabeth, 108 n19

Phillips, Joseph, 108 n19

Pigot, Henry, Major General, 55, 57, *59*

Pitt, William, the Elder, 24

Platt, Mr (Falmouth customs officer), 80

Plymouth: French vessel detained in, 29; packet service removed to (1810), 85–90; telegraph signalling system, 82; women working in, 102; *Chart of Plymouth Sound* (1798), *91*

Pocahontas (ship), 92, 121 n157

Port of London, 17

Post Office: archives, 9; and the capture of the *Prince Adolphus*, 57–8; ceases operation in New York (1775), 53; compensation for loss of packet boats, 60, 99; overseas mail service, 7, 25, 49; packet service taken over by the Admiralty, 100; relations with British military powers, 44–5; seamen's strike (1810), 78–9; West Indies route, 46

postmasters, 16

Powell, Thomas, 107 n9

Prince Adolphus (ship): construction, 53; captured and ransomed off Lisbon, 55–62; West Indies route, 66, 67; incident over Washington Morton's yacht, 74–7; passage to Brazil, 78; seamen's strike (1810), 79–81, 86–7, 89, 90; ownership of, 99, 116 n107; capture by the *Governor McKean*, 92–7, 121 n160; and copper sheathing, 100–1

Prince Ernest (ship), 89

Prince of Wales (ship), 61, 63

Princess Amelia (ship), 95

Princess Elizabeth (ship), 87, 89

privateering, 11, 12–14, 26–7, 49, 92–8

Quallet, Joseph, 110 n33

Queen Charlotte (ship), 89

Quero (ship), 36–7

Rand, Robert, 24, 25, 109 n28

Randlett, Captain, 92, 121 n157

Ratcliff, London, 18, 19, 21, 109 n21

Rich, Edward, 11

Robertson, Archibald, *No 5 of the Circle of Boston, 1776*, 41

Rocque, John, *A plan of the cities of London and Westminster etc* (1746), *18*, *19*, 108 n17

Rogers, Captain, 87, 92–3

Ross, Hugh, 40

Ross, William, 121 n157

Rotherhithe, London, 19, 28, *51*, 66, 68, 110 n33

Also by Sally Jeffery from Turnedup Press:

Dissenting printers: the intractable men and women of a seventeenth-century press

Andrew Sowle was a secret printer. He learned his trade during Cromwell's commonwealth, and practised it under the Stuart restoration. On a hidden press he printed Quaker tracts, illicitly. He survived repeated raids and became the Friends' chief printer and a friend of William Penn. He raised a new generation of printers, most of whom became caught up in the politics of their time. His first apprentice fled to Amsterdam after printing the manifesto of the Duke of Monmouth's doomed rebellion against James II, and may have been William of Orange's campaign printer three years later. One daughter married another apprentice and became notorious for press piracy. Another emigrated to America with her husband, also an ex-apprentice, where they set up the first press in Philadelphia and then fell out with the Quaker leadership there. Andrew's third daughter was herself apprenticed to him as a practical printer, and ran the press in London for over fifty years. A thread of stubborn independence runs through this tribe of printers, who can be tracked through what they published and also in the traces of their collisions with authority.

128 pp hardback, 43 colour illustrations, 5 black and white illustrations
ISBN 978-1-9162221-2-0

Turnedup Press grew out of a blog, *Things turned up by Sally Jeffery while looking for something else*. The author is a typographer who gravitated to writing about printing and other things, in print and online. Some subjects outgrew their territory and turned into books.